Anonymous

The Charter of the Worshipful Company of Poulters, London

Its orders, ordinances, and constitution

Anonymous

The Charter of the Worshipful Company of Poulters, London
Its orders, ordinances, and constitution

ISBN/EAN: 9783337285173

Printed in Europe, USA, Canada, Australia, Japan

Cover: Foto ©Lupo / pixelio.de

More available books at **www.hansebooks.com**

The CHARTER
Of the
Worshipful Company of Poulters,
LONDON;
Its Orders, Ordinances, and Constitution:
ALSO,
ACTS GRANTED BY THE CORPORATION OF LONDON.
With a
LIST *of the* ESTATES *and* CHARITIES *belonging to and under the direction of the* COURT OF ASSISTANTS *of the said* COMPANY.

THE COURT OF ASSISTANTS
OF
The Worshipful Company of Poulters,
LONDON.

Master.
Mr. JAMES LEWIS DOWLING, C.C., Leadenhall Market.

Upper Warden.
Mr. W. R. M. GLASIER, 3, The Paragon, Blackheath, S.E.

Renter Warden.
Alderman Sir P. DE KEYSER, Chatham House, Grove Road, Clapham.

Assistants.
Mr. E. Weatherley, 246, Central Market, P.M.
Mr. Christopher Horne, 44, Auriol Road, West Kensington, P.M.
Mr. F. Dean, 16, Furnival's Inn, P.M.
Mr. Alfred Bays, 18, Marlboro' Road, Old Kent Road, P.M.
Mr. G. T. Sprigens, Leadenhall Market, P.M.
Mr. Wm. Baglehole, 21, Mincing Lane, P.M.
Mr. H. A. Dowse, 6, New Inn, Strand, P.M.
Mr. W. H. Liversidge, Leadenhall Market, P.M.
Mr. W. H. Weatherley, 246, Central Market, P.M.
Mr. Thos. Marsh, Leadenhall Market, P.M.
Mr. Chas. Kynoch, Clunie House, Macaulay Road, Clapham Common, P.M.
Sir Geo. Sherston Baker, Bt., Library Chambers, Temple, P.M.
Mr. Alderman Joseph Savory, Buckhurst Park, Ascot, P.M.
Mr. Geo. F. Brooke, Leadenhall Market, P.M.
Sir Geo. M. Holloway, Tittenhurst, Sunninghill, Berks.

PREFACE.

THE MASTER, WARDENS, and COURT OF ASSISTANTS of the WORSHIPFUL COMPANY of POULTERS being desirous of giving to the Livery of the said Company the proper information respecting the antiquity of the body and the properties in which they are interested, and of which they are Trustees, have printed this Book accordingly.

As early as 1345, the consumption of poultry in London was sufficient to maintain dealers in such feathered ware, for in a patent addressed to the Mayor in the first year of Edward the Third's reign, among other crafts are enumerated, Poulters, Fishmongers, and Butchers (Puleterii, Piscerarii and Carnifices).

In 1345 (19 Edward 3rd), the City Authorities finding that "folks bringing poultry to the City have sold their poultry in lanes, in the hostels of their hosts, and elsewhere in secret, to the great loss and grievance of the citizens," ordained that the poultry should be brought "to the Leaden Hall, and there be sold and no where else," but the residents in the City must not go there, but "sell their property at the stalls (in the Poultry) as of old they were wont to do." "Also, that no cook or regrator shall buy any manner of

Poultry at the Leaden Hall, nor yet at the Stalls before prime rung at the Church of St. Paul, on pain of forfeiting the poultry bought, and going bodily to Prison."

In 1357 the Poulters Freemen of the City were forbidden standing "at the carfukes of the Leden-halle with Rabbits, fowls, or other poultry;" but if they wished to carry them out for sale they must do so "along the wall towards the west of the Church of Saint Michaels on Corn-hulle.

In 1416 (4 Henry 5th) it was ordained that Geese should not be deprived of their giblets by the Poulters, but be sold whole.

The POULTERS COMPANY was incorporated by Royal Charter in the 19th year of the reign of Henry the Seventh, on the 23rd of February, 1504.

It was renewed by Queen Elizabeth on the 22nd February, in the 30th year of her reign.

Charles the Second confirmed it on the 13th June in the 6th year of his reign, and James the Second also confirmed it in the first and last years of his reign.

In the troublous times which then ensued, followed by the Revolution, the original Charter, like most other Charters of the various Companies of the City of London, was lost.

The existing Charter was granted by King William and Queen Mary in the 4th year of their reign on 6th May, 1692. Its orders, ordinances, and constitutions were approved on 19th April the year following.

In the year 1763, "Beckford, Mayor," the Charter was supplemented by an Act of the Corporation of London, and by another Act of the Corporation of London in the year 1820.

The four Documents thus referred to, and a statement of the Estates and Charities belonging to and under the direction of the Court of Assistants of the Worshipful Company of Poulters, were ordered to be printed for the information of the Livery of the Company by a resolution of the Court of Assistants held on the 12th day of January, 1871. The Oaths prescribed by the present Charter to be taken (pp. 53 *et seq.*) are abolished by the Statute 31 and 32 Vic., c. 72. The Promissory Oaths Act 1868, and Declarations to the like effect, are now substituted.

J. L. DOWLING,
MASTER,
December, 1889.

LIST OF PLATE, CHARTERS, &c.

1 Gold and Enamel Jewel, forming the Arms of the Company, presented by the late SIR C. D. CROSLEY, a former Master.

2 small Badges, in Gold and Enamel, forming the Arms of the Company, presented by MR. ALDERMAN SAVORY, a late Master, for use of the Wardens during their office.

1 Silver Flagon, presented by PAST MASTER MR. W. H. LIVERSIDGE.

1 Silver Rosewater Dish, Parcel-gilt, presented by PAST MASTER MR. THOS. MARSH.

1 Silver Punch Bowl, Nepton's Trust Estate, purchased by the Company.

1 Banner, Arms of MR. ALDERMAN SAVORY, presented by him.

1 Banner, Arms of Company, presented by MR. W. H. WEATHERLEY.

1 Arms of the Company, in Silver, framed in Ebony, kept at Clerk's office.

1 large Ebony Hammer, with Arms of Company, in Silver, dated 1662.

1 Beadle's Staff, Bamboo, mounted in Silver, with Arms of Company and a Silver Stork on the top.

The various Charters referred to in the Preface, kept in a box in strong-room under the Guildhall.

The Cloth used by the Court to cover the Table at the Meetings, with the Company's Arms worked thereon, with the date.

William and **Mary** by the Grace of God King and Queen of England Scotland Ffrance and Ireland Defenders of the ffaith **To all** to whom these presents shall come greeting **Whereas** the late Company of Poulters London was an ancient Company and hath enjoyed divers priviledges and immuties by virtue of severall Charters and Letters Patents to them granted by our Royall Predecessors And whereas wee are given to understand that by the late Act of Parliament for reversing the Judgment in a Quo Warranto against the City of London and for restoring the City of London to its antient Rights and Priviledges it is amongst other things enacted that all and every of the severall Companys and Corporations of the said City should from thenceforth stand and be Incorporated by such name and names and in such sort and manner as they respectively were at the time of the said Judgment given And that as well all Surrenders as Charters Letters Patents and Grants for new Incorporating any of the said Companys or touching or concerning any of their Libertys Priviledges or Ffranchises made or granted by the late King James or the King Charles the Second since the giving of the said Judgement should be void and are by the said Act declared null and void **And whereas** at the time of making the said Act there was not a sufficient number left of the former Corporation of Poulters aforesaid to Act as a Company according to their Constitutions Established before the said Judgement given **Know yee** therefore that wee of Our especiall grace certain knowledge and meer motion have Willed Ordained Constituted Granted and Confirmed and by these presents for us our Heirs and Successors do Will Ordaine

Constitute Declare Grant and Confirme that all and singular persons useing the Trade of meere Poulters or selling Poultry Wares Coneys Butter and Eggs within the City of London and Libertys thereof or within seven miles of the same City from time to time for ever hereafter be and shall be by virtue of these presents One Body Corporate and Politick in Deed and name by the name of Master Wardens and Assistants of Poulters London And them by the name of Master Wardens and Assistants of Poulters London Wee do by these presents for us Our Heirs and Successors really and fully make create Ordaine constitute and declare One Body Corporate and Politick in Deed and name And that by the same name of Master Wardens and Assistants of Poulters London they shall and may have perpetuall Succession and that they and their successors by the name of Master Wardens and Assistants of Poulters London shall and may for ever hereafter be persons able and capable in Law to purchase have take receive and enjoy Mannors Messuages Lands Tenements Libertyes priviledges jurisdictions Ffranchizes and other hereditaments whatsoever of whatsoever nature kind or quality they be to them and their successors in ffee and perpetuity or for terme of life or lives year or years or otherwise in what sort soever and also all manner of Goods Chattles and Things whatsoever of what name nature or quality soever they be and also to give grant sell lett alien assigne and dispose of the same Mannors Messuages Lands Tenements Hereditaments Goods Chattels and things aforesaid And that by the same name of Master Wardens and Assistants of Poulters London they shall and may be able to Implead and be Impleaded to Answer and be Answered unto to defend and be defended in all Courts and Places whatsoever and before whatsoever Judges Justices or other persons or Officers of us Our heirs or Successors in all and singular actions Plaints Suits matters and demands of what kind nature or quality soever they be and to Act and do all other matters and things in as ample manner and fforme as any other our Leige Subjects of this our Realme of England being persons able and capable in Law or any other body Politick or Corporate within this our Realme of England can or may have purchase receive possess take and enjoy retain give grant sell lett aliene assigne and dispose plead and be impleaded Answer and be Answered unto defend and be defended do permit and execute And that they the said Master Wardens and Assistants of Poulters London for ever hereafter shall and may have a Common Seale to serve for the Causes and buisness of them and their Successors And that it shall and may be lawfull for them and their Successors to change break alter and make anew the same seale from time to time at their pleasure and as they shall think best And further Wee will and by these presents for us our heirs and Successors do Grant to the said Master Wardens and Assistants of Poulters London and to their Successors that for ever hereafter there shall be one of the Company aforesaid in manner and forme hereafter in these presents mentioned to be chosen and named who shall be and be called the Master of the said Company of Poulters London and that likewise there shall and may be from time to time for ever hereafter two of the said Company in manner and forme hereafter in these presents mentioned to be chosen and named who shall be and be called the Wardens of the Company of Poulters London and also that there shall and may be from time to time for ever hereafter Sixteen others of the Company aforesaid in manner and forme hereafter expressed to be chosen and named who shall be and be called the Assistants of the said Company of Poulters London to be from time to time Assisting and aiding to the Master and Wardens of the said Company for the time being in all causes matters and business touching or concerning the said Company And Wee further will and by these presents for us our heirs and Successors do Grant to the said Master Wardens and Assistants of Poulters London and their Successors that it shall and may be lawfull to and for the said Master Wardens and Assistants of the said Company for the time being or the greater part of them whereof the Master and one of the Wardens for the time being to be always Two as often as they shall think it needful or expedient to assemble Convocate and Congregate themselves together at and in their Hall or any other convenient Place within the said City of London and there from time to time and at all convenient times hereafter to Treat consult determine constitute ordain and make such reasonable Laws Acts orders ordinances and constitutions in writing as to them or the greater part of them then and there assembled whereof the Master and one of the Wardens as aforesaid for the time being to be two shall seem fitt good and convenient according to their best discretion for touching or concerning the good Estate Rule order and Government of the said Company of Poulters London and of every member thereof and in what order and manner the said Master Wardens and Assistants and all and every other person and persons being ffree of the said Company within the Limitts aforesaid shall demeasne and behave themselves as well in all and singular matters causes and things touching or concerning the said Company or anything thereunto appertaining as also the Master Wardens and Assistants in their severall offices Misteries and ffunctions touching and concerning the said Company as aforesaid and all and singular such pains penalties punishments ffines and amerciaments or any of them against or upon any offender or offenders which shall transgress break or violate the said constitutions Statutes Laws ordinances or Orders so to be made Ordained and Established or any of them to impose provide and Limitt and the same and every part and parcel thereof to aske levy take and recover to and for the use of the said Company by way of distress or by Action of debt or otherwise by any other lawfull ways or means against the said Offender or Offenders his her or their goods or chattles or any of them as the Cause shall require and as to the Master Wardens and Assistants of the said Company or the greater part or number of them whereof the Master and one of the Wardens for the time being to be Two shall seem most convenient or expedient All which Laws Orders Ordinances and Constitutions so to be made Ordained and Established as aforesaid Wee will and by these presents for us our heirs and Successors do command to be from time to time and at all times kept obeyed and performed in all things as the same ought to be upon the pains penalties and punishments in the same to be imposed inflicted and Limited so as the same Laws orders Articles and Ordinances paines penaltys ffines and amerciaments be reasonable and not repugnant or contrary but as near as may be agreeable to the Laws and Statutes of this our Realme of England and be first confirmed and approved according to the Statute in that behalfe made and provided And for the better execution of this our Grant in that behalfe Wee have Assigned named constituted and made and by these presents for us our heirs and Successors do assigne create and constitute and make our well-beloved Subject Nathaniell Baldick to be the ffirst and present Master of the said Company of Poulters London to continue in the said office until Ashwednesday now next ensuing the date hereof if the said Nathaniell Baldick shall so long live and from thence untill another of the said Company shall be chosen and named into the said office of Master of the said Company in due manner and fforme according to the Ordinances and provisions hereafter in these presents expressed and mentioned unless the said Nathaniell Baldick shall in the meantime for any notorious fault or misdemeanor or for mis-governement or other just and reasonable Cause be removed from the said office And also wee have assigned named constituted and made and by these presents for us our heirs and Successors Wee doe assigne name constitute and make Our welbeloved Subjects

John Archer and Robert Johnson to be the ffirst and present Wardens of the said Company to continue in the said office of Wardens of the said Company untill Ash Wednesday next ensuing the date hereof if the said John Archer and Robert Johnson or either of them shall so long live and from thence untill Two others of the said Company shall be chosen into the said Offices of Wardens of the said Company of Poulters London according to the Ordinances and Provisions in these presents Expressed and declared unless they the said John Archer and Robert Johnson or either of them shall in the meantime for any notorious fault or misdemeanor or for misgovernement or other just and reasonable cause be removed from the said offices or either of them **And Wee** have also assigned named constituted and made and by these presents for us Our Heirs and Successors Wee do assigne name constitute and make our Welbeloved Subjects Samuell Bishop, John Wybird, Samuel Ball, Henry Kendall, Philip Lemon, Thomas Pusey, John Ffilewood, Richard Pyke, Henry Newdick, Richard Walkden, Leonard Oakes, John Bissell, John Wilkes, Edward Oakely, Ambrose Sheepewash, and William Oliver Citizens and Poulters of the said City of London to be the ffirst and present Assistants of the Company of Poulters London to continue in the said office of Assistants during their severall and respective lives unless they or any of them shall for any notorious fault or misdemeanor or for misgovernement or other just and reasonable cause be removed from the said office of Assistant of the said Company of Poulters London according to the true intent and meaning of these our Letters Patents **And further** wee will and by these presents for us Our Heirs and Successors doe grant to the said Master Wardens and Assistants of Poulters London that the Master Wardens and Assistants or the greater part of them from time to time for ever hereafter shall and may have full power and authority yearly and every year upon Ash Wednesday to nominate elect and choose one of the said Company of Poulters London which shall be Master of the said Company for one whole year from thence next ensuing and from thence untill one other of the said Company shall be chosen and preferred unto the said office of Master of the said Company of Poulters London according to the ordinances and Provisions in these presents expressed and declared and that such person as shall be so chosen and named unto the said office of Master of the said Company before he be admitted to execute the same shall take his corporall oath before the last Precedent Master and Wardens of the said Company or any two of them and before the Assistants for the time being or the greater part of them to execute the said office rightly well and faithfully in all things touching the same and also such other oaths as by the Laws and Statutes of this our Realme are required and that after such oaths soe as aforesaid taken the said person soe elected shall have and exercise the said office of Master of the said Company for One whole year from thence next ensuing and untill one other shall be duely elected and chosen in his place or stead according to the provisions in these presents contained to which last Precedent Master and Wardens for the time being or any two of them Wee doe by these presents for us our Heirs and Successors give and grant full power and authority from time to time to administer the said oaths accordingly and likewise wee doe further for us our heirs and Successors grant and ordaine that at the same time of Electing the said Master as aforesaid the said Master Wardens and Assistants of the said Company for the time being or the greater part of them whereof the Master and one of the Wardens for the time being to be two shall and may also nominate elect and choose two other of the Assistants or of the Livery of the said Company who shall be and shall be called the Wardens of the said Company for one whole year next ensueing and until two others of the Assistants or of the Livery of the said Company be duely chosen elected and sworne unto the said office of Wardens of the said Company according to the ordinances and provisions hereafter declared and expressed and that such persons as shall be so chosen and named unto the said office of Wardens of the said Company before they be admitted to execute the same shall take their respective Corporall oaths before the last Precedent Master and Wardens of the said Company or any two of them for the time being well and truely to execute the said office in all things touching the same and also such other oaths as by the Laws and Statutes of this our Realme are required and that after such oaths so as aforesaid taken the said persons shall and may execute their said offices for one whole year from thence next ensueing and untill Two others shall be duely elected and chosen in their places and steads according to the provisions in these presents contained to which said last Precedent Master and Wardens or any two of them for the time being **Wee** do by these presents for us our heirs and Successors give and grant full power and authority from time to time to administer the same oaths accordingly **And** further wee will and by these presents for us our Heirs and Successors do grant to the said Master Wardens and Assistants of Poulters London and to their Successors that if it shall happen the Master Wardens or Assistants of the said Company for the time being or any of them at any time after they shall be elected and chosen into his or their office or offices to dye or be removed from his or their office or offices which said Master Wardens and Assistants and every of them for Ill Government or for any other just or reasonable cause Wee will from time to time shall be removed by the greater part of the Master Wardens and Assistants of the Company aforesaid for the time being that then and so often it shall and may be lawfull to and for such and so many of the said Master Wardens and Asssistants which shall be then liveing or remaining or the greater part of them at their pleasures to choose and make one

THE WORSHIPFUL COMPANY OF POULTERS. 9

other of the said Company to be Master and one or more others of the said Company to be Warden or Wardens Assistant or Assistants of the said Company the same person or persons to be chosen out of the Livery and Freemen of the said Company according to the Ordinances and Provisions before in these presents expressed and declared to execute the said office of Master or Office or Offices of Warden or Wardens untill Ash Wednesday then next following and from thenceforth untill others shall be chosen in their places as aforesaid and so as often as the case shall require and the said person or persons so to be chosen Assistant or Assistants to execute the said office or offices of Assistant or Assistants of the said Company for and during their respective naturall Lives unless such person or persons shall be removed in manner and forme above expressed Neberthelesss wee will that every Master Warden and Assistant of the said Company to be nominated and elected in the place or places of him or them so dying or being removed from time to time for ever hereafter before he or they shall be admitted to the execution of the said office or offices shall take his and their corporall oath before the Master Wardens and Assistants for the time being or the greater part of them well rightly and faithfully to Execute the said office in and by all things respectively touching and concerning the same and also such other oaths as by the Laws and Statutes of this Our Realme are required to which said Master Wardens and Assistants for the time being or the greater part of them Wee do by these presents for us our Heirs and Successors give and grant full power and authority from time to time as often as occasion shall require to administer such oath and oaths accordingly And further wee will and by these presents for us our Heirs and Successors do grant and ordaine for the better Order Rule and Government of all and singular person and persons which now are or hereafter shall be free of the said Company of Poulters London that the said Master Wardens and Assistants of the said Company for the time being for ever shall have the View Oversight Search correction and Government of all and singular persons whatsoever of the said Company and of the Wares goods and Commodityes by them or any of them sold or offered to be put to sale and that the said Master Wardens and Assistants or the Major part of them shall have power and Authority by virtue of these presents and according to the Laws and Constitutions aforesaid to punish and correct and cause to be punished and corrected Offenders for their offences deceits abuses or misdemeanors in the occupation or use of the said Trade of meere Poulters 𝔄𝔫𝔡 Wee Will and by these presents for us our Heirs and Successors do straightly charge and command all and singular Mayors Justices Sheriffs Constables and all other the Officers Ministers and Subjects of us our Heirs and Successors that they and every of them be aiding helping and assisting to the Master Wardens and Assistants of Poulters London for the time being to doe enjoy have and execute all and singular thing and things whatsoever by us before in these presents granted unto them or to be used or exercised by the said Master Wardens and Assistants or any of them and every or any part and parcell thereof according to the true intent and meaning of these presents 𝔄𝔫𝔡 𝔣𝔲𝔯𝔱𝔥𝔢𝔯 𝔨𝔫𝔬𝔴 𝔜𝔢𝔢 that Wee of our especiall grace certain knowledge and meere motion and for the better maintenance of the said Master Wardens and Assistants and supporting the necessary charges of the said Company have given and granted and by these presents for us our heirs and Successors doe give and grant unto the said Master Wardens and Assistants of Poulters London and their Successors speciall License and ffree and lawful power and authority to have take purchase receive enjoy and possess to them and their Successors for ever any Lordships Mannors Messuages Lands Tenements Meadows Pastures ffeedings Woods Underwoods Rectories Tythes Rents Reversions and other hereditaments whatsoever as well of us Our heirs or Successors as of any other person or persons whatsoever so as the said Mannors Messuages Lands Tenements and other hereditaments do not exceed in the whole the yearly value of Fforty pounds above all deductions and reprises 𝕬𝖓𝖉 𝖋𝖚𝖗𝖙𝖍𝖊𝖗 Wee have given and granted and by these presents for us Our Heirs and Successors do give and grant unto all and every the subjects whatsoever of us our Heirs and Successors speciall License and ffree and lawfull power and authority that he they or any of them shall and may give grant sell sett alien lett or demise unto the Master Wardens and Assistants of Poulters London and their Successors any Lordships Mannors Messuages Rectories Tithes Lands Tenements Rents Reversions and other Hereditaments whatsoever so as the Lordships Mannors Messuages Lands Tenements and other Hereditaments so to be given granted aliened sold or conveyed to the said Master Wardens and Assistants of Poulters London do not in the whole exceed the yearly value of Fforty pounds above all deductions and reprises 𝕬𝖓𝖉 𝖆𝖑𝖘𝖔 Wee will and by these presents for us our Heirs and Successors do grant unto the said Master Wardens and Assistants and their Successors full power and authority that the Master Wardens and Assistants of the said Company for the time being or the greater part of them shall and may from time to time name elect choose and constitute one fitt and meet person to be Clerke of the said Company to serve for the affairs of the said Company and two other fitt and meet persons to be Beadles of the said Company to be serviceable and attendant on the said Master Wardens and Assistants of the said Company and all matters touching the same and the said Clerke and Beadles and every of them for reasonable and just cause to displace and remove and other persons in their place or places at the discretion of the Master Wardens

B

and Assistants or greater part of them for the time being to choose and elect which said Clerke and Beadles so elected and Ordained before they be admitted to the executing of their said Offices shall take their Corporall oaths before the Master Wardens and Assistants of the said Company for the time being or the greater part of them well faithfully and honestly to demean and behave themselves in the execution of the said Offices respectively and such other oaths as by the Laws and Statutes of this our Realme are required to which said Master Wardens and Assistants or the greater part of them for the time being for us our heirs and Successors Wee do hereby give power and authority to administer such like Oaths as well to the aforesaid Clerke and Beadles as to all other persons which from time to time shall be admitted into the said Company and for the better prevention of severall inconveniencies in the said Trade and the selling of bad unwholesome and deceiptfull Poultry Wares Wee will and by these presents for us our Heirs and Successors do ordaine and firmely charge and command that no person or persons whatsoever from henceforth within our said City of London and seven Miles Compass of the same do use exercise or practise the said Trade of meere Poulters or selling Poultry Wares or Coneys unless he or they shall first have served as an apprentice or apprentices to the said Mistery of a Poulter for the space of seven years at the least according to the Statute in that behalf made and provided and shall be admitted a ffreeman of the said Company of Poulters London upon pain of being proceeded against for their Contempts thereof according to the Laws and Statutes of this our Realme **And further** Wee will and by these presents for us our Heirs and Successors do hereby authorise and command the Master Wardens and Assistants of the said Company for the time being to admit to the ffreedom of the said Company every person and persons that now have served or hereafter shall serve as an apprentice to the said trade of Poulter by the space of seven years within the said City of London or seven miles of the same and shall desire to be admitted a ffreeman of the said Company he or they paying unto the said Master and Wardens of the said Company for the use of the said Company two shillings and six pence for his or their admission to be a ffreeman of the said Company And Wee further will and by these presents for us our Heirs and Successors do hereby Authorise and Command the Master Wardens and Assistants of the said Company for the time being from time to time to take care that all the Laws and Statutes made and to be made for and concerning Poultry Wares be put in full and due execution upon any offender or offenders being a Member or Members of the said Company in all things according to the Tenor and purport of the same Laws and Statutes respectively And it is our Royall will and pleasure and Wee do hereby for us our heirs and Successors give and grant unto the said Master Wardens and Assistants of Poulters London and their Successors that they or the Major part of them whereof the Master and one of the Wardens for the time being to be two shall and may from time to time hereafter elect and choose in manner and forme aforesaid out of the Livery of the said Company such and so many person and persons to be Assistant and Assistants of the said Company as in their discretion shall seem fitt so as the persons so elected do not encrease the Assistants of the said Company to any more than Two and Twenty in number at any one time which said person and persons so to be elected or chosen Assistants of the said Company shall take such oath and oaths and shall continue in the said office of Assistants and shall be removeable from the said office in such manner and forme as is hereinbefore mentioned touching and concerning the other Assistants hereinbefore appointed And further of our more ample grace certain knowledge and meere motion Wee have granted ratifyed and confirmed And by these presents for us our Heirs and Successors do grant ratifye and confirme unto the said Master Wardens and Assistants of Poulters London and their Successors all and every the Lands Tenements Rents Revenues Hereditaments Customs powers Authorities Immunitys Exemptions Priviledges Ffranchises Sume and Sumes of money and Duties commonly called Quarteradges Profits Emoluments Rights Credits goods and Chattles whatsoever of what nature kind or quality which the Master Wardens and Assistants of the Company of Poulters London or any of them by whatsoever name or names of Incorporation or by whatsoever other lawful ways or means at any time or times heretofore have had used or enjoyed or which they or any of them ought to have use and enjoy by virtue of any Charters or Letters Patents of any of our Royall predecessors Kings or Queens of England made granted or confirmed and which were in force at the time of the said Judgment given by virtue of any lawfull Custome Ordinance Constitution use Prescription or other right or Title whatsoever **To have** and to hold all and singular the said Lands Hereditaments and premises aforesaid unto the said Master Wardens and Assistants of Poulters London and their Successors for ever **Yielding** and paying therefore unto us our Heirs and Successors yearly such and the like Rents services sumes of money and demands as heretofore have been or of right ought to be paid or Answered for the same **And lastly** our Will and pleasure is that the said NATHANIELL BALDICKE herein named to be first and present Master of the said Company before he enter upon the execution of his said office do take the oaths herein appointed to be taken by the Master of the said Company for the time being before the said JOHN ARCHER and ROBERT JOHNSON and that the said JOHN ARCHER and ROBERT JOHNSON herein named to be the first and present Wardens of the said Company before they enter upon the Execution of their said offices do severally take the oaths hereinbefore appointed to be taken by the Wardens of the said Company for the time being before the said NATHANIELL BALDICKE and that the several persons above named to be the ffirst and present Assistants of the said Company before they or any of them enter upon the execution of their respective offices of Assistants do severally take the oaths herein appointed to be taken by the Assistants of the said Company for the time being before the said present Master and Wardens or any two of them whereof the said Master to be one To which said Master and Wardens respectively We do hereby give full power and Authority to administer the said severall and respective oaths accordingly **In Witnesse** whereof Wee have caused these our Letters to be made Patents **Witnesse** Ourselves at Westminster the sixth day of May in the fourth yeare of our Reigne

By Writt of Privy Seale   PIGOTT

Pro fine in Hanaperio sex Libr Tresdecem solid et quatuor denarios
I. TREVOR S.
G HUTCHINSES

Orders Ordinances and Constitutions made the thirteenth day of May Anno Domini One thousand Six hundred ninety two and in the fourth yeare of the Reigne of Our Sovereign Lord and Lady William and Mary by the Grace of God of England Scotland Ffrance and Ireland King and Queene Defenders of the ffaith By the Master Wardens and Assistants of Poulters London for touching and concerning the good Estate Rule order and Government of the said Company of Poulters London and the members thereof

Memorandum It is ordained ordered and Established by the said Masters Wardens and Assistants of Poulters London And the said Master

Wardens and Assistants of Poulters London doe ordain order and establish in manner and forme following that is to say.

1 **Imprimis** It is ordained and established by the said Master Wardens and Assistants that yearly and every yeare upon the day called Ash Wednesday for ever hereafter the Master Wardens and Assistants of the said Company of Poulters London shall Assemble and meet together at such time and place as the Master of the said Company for the time being shall appoint to elect and choose a Master and two Wardens for the said Company for the yeare then next ensuing which day called Ash Wednesday shall for ever hereafter be called Electionday.

2 **Item** That yearly upon the said Electionday for ever there shall be named by the Master Wardens and Assistants of the said Company of Poulters London for the time being or the more part of them whereof the Master of the said Company for the time being to be One Two of the Assistants of the said Company and noe other to be in Election to be Master or the said Company for the yeare then next following of which two persons soe to be named the Master Wardens and Assistants of the said Company for the time being then being present shall by their severall votes to be sett downe in writing nominate One to be Master of the said Company for the yeare then next ensuing And that he of the said two Assistants who then shall have the most votes shall be imediately declared to be and shall be Master of the said Company for the yeare then next following and from thence untill another Master shall be named Elected chosen and sworne if he shall or doe so long live and be not in the mean season removed for any misgovernement or other Misdemeanour or just or

reasonable cause and if any person being Master shall at any time hereafter dye or be removed as aforesaid from his said office that then and so often within ten days next after the death or removall of every such Master there shall be one other person named elected and chosen in manner and forme aforesaid to be Master of the said Company in the Roome and place of him so dead or removed which person so elected and chosen shall be and continue Master of the said Company untill the Generall Electionday then next following and from thence untill one other shall be chosen and sworne Master of the said Company.

3 **Item** That yearly upon the said Election day for ever hereafter presently after the Master is chosen there shall be named by the Master Wardens and Assistants of the said Company for the time being or by the more part of them ffour persons being then of the Livery of the said Company for the yeare then next following of which four persons so to be named the Master Wardens and Assistants of the said Company for the time being then being present shall by their severall Votes to be sett downe in Writing nominate two to be Wardens of the said Company for the yeare then next ensueing and that those two who then shall have most Votes shall be imediately declared to be and shall be Wardens of the said Company for the yeare then next ensueing and from thence untill other Wardens shall be named elected chosen and Sworne in manner and forme as aforesaid if they do and shall so long live and be not in the meane season removed for any mis-government or other mis-demeanour or just or reasonable Cause And if any person being Warden of the said Company shall at any time hereafter dye or be removed as aforesaid from his said office That then and so often within ten days next

after the death or removeall of every such Warden there shall be one other person of the Livery of the said Company named in manner and forme aforesaid to be one of the Wardens of the said Company in the roome or place of him so dead or removed which person soe elected and chosen shall be and Continue one of the Wardens of the said Company until the generall election day then next following and from thence till others shall be named elected chosen and Sworne Wardens of the said Company.

4 **Item** That every person and persons that hereafter shall be elected or chosen to be Master or Warden of the said Company with all convenient speed after he or they shall be so elected and chosen and before he or they take his or their place or places or execute his or their Office or Offices shall take the respective Oath and Oaths of their respective place or places Office and Offices hereafter mentioned in manner following that is to say the said person so as aforesaid chosen to be Master of the said Company before the Master and Wardens of the said Company for the time being or any two of them and the greater part of the Assistants of the said Company for the time then being shall in due forme of Law take the oath of Master of the said Company hereafter mentioned and the said persons so as aforesaid chosen to be Wardens of the said Company shall before the Master and Wardens of the said Company for the time being or any two of them whereof the Master of the said Company for the time being shall be one in due forme of Law take the oath hereafter mentioned of Warden and Wardens of the said Company.

5 **Item** If any person or persons that now is or are or hereafter shall be of the Assistants of the said Company shall happen to dye or be

removed by the Master Wardens and Assistants of the said Company for the time being for any misgovernement or other misdemeanour in his or their office or offices of Assistant or Assistants of the said Company for any just or reasonable cause   That then and so often the said Master Wardens and Assistants of the said Company for the time being or the more part of them whereof the Master for the time being to be one shall within tenn days after the death or removeall as aforesaid of any such Assistant or Assistants elect and choose one or more person or persons of the Livery of the said Company to be Assistant or Assistants of the said Company in the Roome and place of such person or persons as shall so die or be removed as aforesaid which person or persons so chosen as aforesaid to be Assistant or Assistants of the said Company before he or they shall and doe take upon him or them or doe or shall execute the said office or offices of Assistant or Assistants of the said Company shall in due forme of Law take the oath hereafter mentioned of Assistant or Assistants of the said Company before the Master and Wardens of the said Company for the time being or the more part of them whereof the Master of the said Company for the time being to be one which person or persons soe chosen or to be chosen and duely sworne Assistant or Assistants of the said Company shall continue in the said office or offices of Assistant and Assistants of the said Company during his naturall life unless he or they shall be removed from the said office or offices of Assistant or Assistants of the said Company for misgovernement or other misdemeanour in the said Company or for any other just or reasonable cause   And that every one who now is or hereafter shall be of the Livery of the said Company that shall be elected and chosen as aforesaid to be one of the said Assistants of the said Company not haveing formerly been elected to be one of the Assistants of the said Company shall for his admission into the office of Assistant of the said Company pay unto the Master and Wardens of the said Company for the time being to and for the use of the said Company the sume of Ffive pounds of good and lawfull money of England and to the Clerke of the said Company for the time being for entering his admittance and giveing him his oath ffive shillings and to the Upper Beadle of the said Company for the time being two shillings and to the Under Beadle twelve pence And if such person so chosen as aforesaid to be one of the Assistants of the said Company shall not within tenn days next after his admission into the said office of one of the Assistants of the said Company well and truely pay or cause to be paid unto the Master and Wardens of the said Company for the time being the said Ffive pounds to and for the use of the said Company that then such person shall forfeit and loose for such his neglect to the Master and Wardens of the said Company for the time being to and for the use of the said Company the sume of Six pounds thirteen shillings and fourpence of like lawfull money of England.

6 **Item** That if any person being ffree of the said Company that shall at any time or times hereafter be elected and chosen to be either Master or One of the Wardens or Assistants of the said Company shall after due notice given to him of such his Election neglect by the space of ten days or shall deny or refuse to take upon him such of the said offices respectively as he shall be elected and chosen into as aforesaid or to take the oath hereafter mentioned and appointed to be taken by such officer not then haveing such a just cause or reasonable lett or impediment to excuse such his neglect denyall or refuseall as by the Master Wardens and Assistants of the said Company for the time being or the more part of them whereof the Master of the said Company for the time being to be one shall be thought and adjudged sufficient shall for every such neglect refuseall or deniall forfeite and pay to the Master Wardens and Assistants

of the said Company for the time being to and for the use of the said Company the sumes of money hereafter mentioned that is to say every one who shall neglect deny or refuse as aforesaid to accept and take upon him the office of Master of the said Company the sume of Ffifteen pounds of good and lawfull money of England and every one who shall neglect denye or refuse as aforesaid to accept and take upon him the office of One of the Wardens of the said Company the sume of Tenn pounds of good and lawfull money of England and every one who shall as aforesaid neglect refuse or deny to accept and take upon him the office of one of the Assistants of the said Company the sume of Twenty pounds of lawfull money of England Provided always and It is further ordained and established by the Master Wardens and Assistants of the said Company that every one that shall be elected and chosen to be one of the Assistants of the said Company and shall as aforesaid neglect refuse or deny to take upon him the said office of one of the Assistants of the said Company and shall pay the said ffine or sume of Twenty pounds to and for the use of the said Company shall from and after the payment of such ffine be for ever afterwards ffreed and discharged of and from bearing or being elected into any other office or offices in the said Company.

7 Item That every one of the Assistants of the said Company for the time being and every other person or persons being of the Livery of the said Company upon the said generall election day and upon every other day appointed for the election and choice of any Master or Wardens of the said Company upon warneing and notice thereof unto him or them given or left in writing for him or them at his or their then habitation or habitations by the Beadle of the said Company for the time being shall make his and their personall appearance in their Liverys at the Comon Hall of the said Company or at such convenient place as the then Master

and Wardens shall appoint That is to say the said Assistants at or before the hour of 8 o'clock in the forenoon of every of the same days and every other person and persons being of the Livery of the said Company at or before the hour of 9 of the clock in the forenoon of every of the same days And after a new Master and new Wardens for the said Company shall be chosen shall upon the said Generall election day in a decent and comely manner and in their Liveries attend on the said new Master and Wardens to such Church as shall be assigned by the said new Master and Wardens then and there to hear Divine service and there shall continue and abide during the time of Divine service and after Divine service ended shall likewise attend the said New Master and Wardens in a decent and comely manner and in their Liveries from the Church to the Hall of the said Company or to such other convenient place as the said New Master and Wardens shall appoint and from thence without a reasonable cause shall not depart till he or they shall be Licensed so to do by the Master and Wardens then being And that every person being warned as aforesaid that shall come after the respective hour or hours shall forfeit and pay unto the Master Wardens and Assistants of the said Company for the time being to and for the use of the said Company for his late comeing twelve pence And if he shall not attend in forme aforesaid he shall forfeit and pay unto the Master Wardens and Assistants of the said Company for the time being to and for the use of the said Company for every such offence ffive shillings and if he depart without License he shall forfeit and pay to the said Master Wardens and Assistants of the said Company for the time being to and for the use of the said Company for every such departure two shillings.

8 **Item** That the Master Wardens and Assistants of the said Company for the time being or the more part of them from time to time and

at all times hereafter when and so often as they shall think convenient and find it needfull shall and may call nominate choose and admit unto the Livery or Cloathing of the said Company such and so many person and persons being ffreemen of the said Company as they shall think meet honest and of Ability to be called and admitted into the same Livery and that every such person soe called and chosen shall thereupon pay to the Master Wardens and Assistants of the said Company for the time being to and for the use of the said Company for his admission into the Livery of the said Company the sume of Twenty pounds of lawfull money of England to be employed according to the custome and usage of the said City of London   And shall also pay to the Clerke of the said Company for the time being for the Entring and Registring his name in the Books of the said Company the sume of Ffive shillings and to the upper Beadle of the said Company for the time being the sume of 1s 6d and to the under Beadle twelve pence   And that every person that shall be so called elected and chosen into the Livery and shall refuse or deny to be of the same Livery not having any such lawfull just or reasonable cause or lett to excuse such his refusall or deniall as by the Master Wardens and Assistants of the said Company for the time being or the more part of them whereof the Master of the said Company for the time being to be one shall be thought and adjudged sufficient shall for every time of such his refuseall or denial forfeit and pay to the Master Wardens and Assistants of the said Company for the time being to and for the use of the said Company the sume of Tenn pounds of good and lawfull money of England unless he shall before the Master and Wardens of the said Company for the time being or the more part of them whereof the Master of the said Company for the time being to be one in due forme of Law take his corporall Oath that he is not bona fide worth the sume of one hundred and fifty markes.

9 **Item** For as much as decent and comely apparel is to be used by the citizens of so noble a City as London is It is therefore ordered that the Master and Wardens of the said Company for the time being shall at all times hereafter sit and be cloathed in a Gowne of fines in all and every their Court and Courts or other Assemblies in their Common Hall or other convenient place to be appointed by the Master and Wardens of the said Company for the time being for such Assemblies And that every person now being or that hereafter shall be of the Livery of the said Company shall from time to time hereafter come and be present before the Master and Wardens of the said Company for the time being when they shall be setting in the said Hall or other convenient place to be appointed as aforesaid in any Court or other Assembly of the said Master and Wardens of the said Company for the time being about the business of the said Company and at all other times when and so often as the said Company shall or ought to attend in their Liveries for any reasonable cause whatsoever shall come before and attend the Master Wardens and Assistants of the said Company for the time being in a Gowne And that every person that shall offend or do contrary to any part of this Ordinance shall forfeit and pay to the Master Wardens and Assistants of the said Company for the time being to and for the use of the said Company for every such offence Ffive shillings of good and lawfull money of England.

10 **Item** That the Master and Assistants of the said Company for the time being or the more part of them whereof the Master of the said Company for the time being to be one shall and may from time to time as often as occasion shall require elect and choose out of those that shall be Wardens of the said Company one to be the Renter Warden for the yeare then next ensuing And that every such

Renter Warden shall when and so soon as he hath received the moneys plate goods and Stock of the said Company or any part thereof into his hands or Custody enter into one Bond or Obligation with such a sufficient Surety or Suretys if a Surety or Suretys shall be required the same surety or Suretys not to be a member or members of the said Company in such penalty and to such person or persons as the Master and Assistants of the said Company for the time being or the more part of them whereof the Master of the said Company for the time being to be One shall direct accept and approve of with condition to give unto the Master and Assistants for the time being of the said Company or to the more part of them whereof the Master of the said Company for the time being to be one upon every Court day if thereunto required or otherwise when the Master and Assistants of the said Company for the time being or the more part of them shall demand the same a just true and particular accompt of all moneys received and paid by him or to him for or on the behalfe or upon the account of the said Company And that every such Renter Warden of the said Company for the time being shall if thereunto required upon every Court day give and render unto the Master and Assistants of the said Company for the time being or the more part of them whereof the Master of the said Company for the time being to be one a just and true account of all moneys by him received or paid upon account of the said Company and of all other matters relating to the said office And that if any person so elected and chosen to be Renter Warden shall deny or refuse to take upon him the place of Renter Warden of the said Company not haveing any such just or reasonable cause of excuse as the Master and Assistants of the said Company for the time being or the more part of them whereof the Master of the said Company for the time being to be one shall allow and approve of that then he shall forfeit and pay to the Master and Assistants of the said Company for the time being to and for the use of the said Company for such his refuseall the sume of Tenn pounds of good and lawfull money of England And also that if such person so elected and chosen Renter Warden of the said Company after he hath accepted of the said Office shall neglect or refuse to make and give such Bond as aforesaid That then for such his refuseall or neglect he shall forfeit and loose his said office and also shall pay unto the Master Wardens and Assistants of the said Company for the time being to and for the use of the said Company the sume of Twenty pounds of good and lawfull money of England And further that if such Renter Warden after he hath accepted and taken on him the said Office shall neglect or refuse being thereunto required by the Master of the said Company for the time being to give a just and true account as aforesaid that then for every such neglect or refuseall he shall forfeit and pay to the Master and Assistants of the said Company for the time being to and for the use of the said Company the sume of fforty shillings of good and lawfull money of England **Provided** and it is ordained and established that no account of any such Renter Warden of the said Company shall be allowed by the Auditors of the said Company for the time being unless all such Sume and Sumes of money as shall be therein mentioned to have been paid or expended by such Renter Warden shall be paid and expended for the just and necessary occasions and business and affairs of the said Company and unless it shall be expressed in the said account when and to whome and for what cause or occasion such sume or sumes of money were paid or expended.

11 **Item** It is ordained and Established that the Master Wardens

and Assistants of the said Company for the time being shall not at any time hereafter directly or indirectly give grant bargaine sell or otherwise doe away any Lands tenements or hereditaments that to the said Company now do or hereafter shall belong or appertaine nor make any Lease or Grant thereof in Reversion or Reversions nor for any longer terme than for one and Twenty years in possession nor for any lesse Rent than the old and accustomed Rent thereof without the consent of the said Company or the more part of them that upon notice given of a meeting appointed by the Master Wardens and Assistants of the said Company for the time being or the more part of them to be had and held by the said Company shall at such meeting be assembled

12 Item That the Master Wardens and Assistants of the said Company for the time being or the more part of them whereof the Master of the said Company for the time being to be one shall and may from time to time and at all times hereafter when and as often as need shall require elect and choose one honest wise and discreet and fitt person to be a Clerk to the Master Wardens and Assistants of the said Company for the time being and to give them advice and councell in their affairs and business and to keep their Courts and to enter and Register their accounts and generally to doe and execute all that and whatsoever which to the office of the Clerk of the Master Wardens and Assistants of the said Company for the time being doth and shall appertain And that every person so elected and chosen to be Clerk before he take upon him that office shall before the Master and Wardens of the said Company for the time being be Sworne and take the oath of Clerk of the said Company hereafter mentioned And that every person so elected chosen and sworne Clerk as aforesaid

shall and may thenceforth have hold execute use and enjoy the same office and also have hold receive perceive take and enjoy all and every the ffee and ffees commodityes and profits thing and things whatsoever to the same office in anywise appertaining or belonging or thereunto united or annexed unless he for some just cause shall be removed and put from the said office by the Master Wardens and Assistants of the said Company for the time being or the more part of them whereof the Master of the said Company for the time being to be One

13 **Item** That the Master Wardens and Assistants of the said Company for the time being or the more part of them whereof the Master of the said Company for the time being to be one shall or may from time to time and at all times hereafter when and as often as need shall require elect and choose one or more honest discret and fitt person or persons to be Beadle or Beadles to the Master Wardens and Assistants of the said Company for the time being to serve them and to be attendant upon the Master and Wardens of the said Company for the time being and at their lawfull comandment concerning the affairs and business of the said Company and Generally to doe and execute all that and whatsoever which to the office of Beadle or Beadles of the said Company doe and shall appertaine and that every person and persons so elected and chosen to be Beadle or Beadles of the said Company as aforesaid before he or they take upon him or themselves that office shall before the Master and Wardens of the said Company for the time being be sworne and take the oath of Beadle of the said Company which oath is hereafter mentioned and expressed and that every person so elected and sworne Beadle as aforesaid shall or may from thenceforth have use

execute and enjoy the said office and also have hold receive take and enjoy all and every the ffee or ffees commodityes profits thing and things whatsoever to the same office in anywise appertaining or belonging or thereunto united or annexed unless he or they shall be removed from the said office by the Master Wardens and Assistants of the said Company for the time being or the more part of them whereof the Master of the said Company for the time being to be one for any just or reasonable cause

14 Item That the Master Wardens and Assistants of the said Company for the time being or the more part of them whereof the Master and one of the Wardens of the said Company for the time being to be two shall or may hereafter keep and hold in the Common Hall of the said Company or in any other Convenient place to be appointed by the Master and Wardens of the said Company for the time being Two half yearly Courts that is to say one within twenty days next after the ffeast of the Nativity of Saint John the Baptist and the other within twenty days next after the ffeast of the Birth of Our Lord Christ for ever And that the Beadle or Beadles of the said Company for the time being shall by the Commandment of the Master and Wardens of the said Company for the time being or any two of them whereof the Master of the said Company for the time being to be one shall summon or warne all and every person and persons whatsoever useing or exerciseing or that shall use or exercise the said Art or Mistery of Poulters within the City of London Suburbs or Libertyes thereof or within seven miles of the same City and also all and every person and persons being ffree of the said Company to be and appear at the said severall and respective Courts and then and there to pay their Quarteridge shall continue at the

said Court during such time as such of the orders of the said Company shall be read as the Master and Wardens of the said Company for the time being or the more part of them shall think fitt and appoint to be read And that if any of the said persons that shall be so sumoned to be at either of the said half yearly Courts shall not appear at the said Courts or any of them but shall be absent from the same or any of them not haveing such a just Cause or reasonable lett to excuse his absence as by the Master Wardens and Assistants of the said Company for the time being or the more part of them whereof the Master of the said Company for the time being to be one shall be thought and adjudged sufficient shall for every time of such his absence forfeit and pay to the Master Wardens and Assistants of the said Company for the time being to and for the use of the said Company the sume of Six shillings and eight pence of good and lawfull money of England

15 **Item** That the Master Wardens and Assistants of the said Company for the time being or the more part of them whereof the Master and one of the Wardens of the said Company for the time being to be two shall hereafter for ever upon every ffirst Friday in every month in the yeare keep and hold at the Comon Hall of the said Company or other convenient place to be appointed by the Master and Wardens of the said Company a Court of Assistants for the handling conferring consulting counselling and determining of and about these present Articles constitutions and ordinances and such other articles Constitutions and ordinances as heretofore have been made ordained or hereafter shall be made by the Master Wardens and Assistants of the said Company for the time being for the good government of the said Company and the well ordering of the said Art and Mistery and of

the Members of the said Company and for the hearing adjudgeing deciding ending and determining of all ffines amerciaments Misdemeanours Controversies and debates whatsoever touching and concerning the said Company and the members thereof and the said Art or Mistery and touching and concerning these present ordinances or orders or any other ordinances or orders of or concerning the said Company heretofore or hereafter to be made or touching or concerning any person or persons useing or exerciseing the said art or Mistery within the said City of London Libertyes or Suburbs thereof or within 7 miles of the same City and that to be at every or any of the same Courts there shall or may be summoned by the Beadle or Beadles of the said Company for the time being at or by the Commandment of the Master and Wardens of the said Company for the time being or any two of them whereof the Master of the said Company for the time being to be one All and every person and persons that then hath or have or that then is or shall be accused or suspected to have committed or done any Act or Acts thing or things whatsoever contrary to any of the Ordinances Decrees orders and constitutions herein contained and that every person that shall so be summoned to be at any of the said Courts and doth not come accordingly but maketh default and is absent from any of the said Courts and hath not then such a just cause or reasonable lett to excuse for his absence as by the Master Wardens and Assistants of the said Company for the time being or the more part of them whereof the Master of the said Company for the time being to be one shall be thought and adjudged sufficient shall for every time of such his absence pay to the Master Wardens and Assistants of the said Company for the time being to and for the use of the said Company the sume of three shillings and ffour pence of good and lawfull money of England **Provided** always and it is hereby ordained that if the Master shall refuse or neglect to call a Court as aforesaid It shall be lawfull for the Wardens or

Warden to call a Court and with the major part of that Court to Elect a new Master in the place of him so neglecting or refuseing to do as aforesaid And that he shall not onely be removed from his place but shall pay such summe or summs of money as if he had fined for the said office according to the Laws and Orders in that behalfe made

16 **Item** That noe lisence given by any Master or Wardens of the said Company for the time being to any person to be absent from any half-yearly Court or Courts of Assistants or other Court day or days appointed as aforesaid for the meeting of the said Company shall be allowed of Except such Master or Warden giveing License be himself present at the same Court or day appointed for the meeting of the said Company to Witness the Lisence and leave by him given And that the Master and Wardens soe giveing lisence shall presently pay all such Quarteridge and other ffines as the same person to whome such leave is given ought to pay if he had appeared himself in person upon paine to forfeit and pay to the Master Wardens and Assistants of the said Company for the time being to and for the use of the said Company the summe of tenn shillings of good and lawfull money of England

17 **Item** If it shall happen that either by reason of sickness or of any other Urgent or Important occasion the Master of the said Company for the time being cannot be himself present in person at any half-yearly Court or Courts of Assistants That then and in such case it shall and may be lawfull to and for the Assistants of the said Company for the time being or the more part of them then present to nominate and appoint one of the Wardens or Assistants of the said Company for the time being or the more part of them that shall be then present to be in the Chaire and supplying the place of such Master of the said Company in his absence which

said person so to be nominated shall have full power and authority to doe execute and performe all and every such Act and Acts thing and things and in as large and ample manner in every respect as the Master for the time being might or could do if he were personally present

18 Item Whereas their Majesties that now are by their letters Patents under the Great Seale of England have granted to the said Company the selling of Butter and Eggs within the City of London Suburbs and Liberties thereof or within seven miles thereof as being part of the Trade of Poulters It is therefore ordained constituted and established that every person and persons that now are or hereafter shall be free of the said Company and all other person and persons not being ffree of the said Company and useing and exerciseing the said Arts or Mistery and all Livery men Journeymen and other person and persons selling or that shall hereafter sell any Butter or Eggs within the said City of London Suburbs and Libertyes thereof or within seven Miles thereof shall pay to the Master Wardens and Assistants of the said Company for the time being to and for the use of the said Company the yearly sume of two shillings of good and lawfull money of England at the ffeasts of Saint Michael the Archangell the Birth of Our Lord Christ the Annunciation of the Blessed Virgin Mary and the Nativity of Saint John the Baptist by equall and even portions and that every of the said persons who shall wilfully neglect to or upon demand thereof shall deny or refuse or faile to make payment thereof shall forfeit and pay to the Master Wardens and Assistants of the said Company for the time being To and for the use of the said Company for every such neglect refusall deniall or failure of payment the sume of fforty shillings of Lawfull money of England

19 Item To the End and intent to prevent as much as possible

may be That noe unwholesome Poultry Wares Butter Eggs or Coneys may be sold uttered or put to sale within the said City of London Suburbs or Liberties thereof or within seven Miles of the same It is ordained and established that the Master Wardens and Assistants of the said Company for the time being or any four of them whereof the Master and one of the Wardens of the said Company for the time being to be two shall and may have full power and authority from time to time and at all times hereafter when and as often as they shall please and see occasion for it to search and oversee the Butter Eggs and Coneys and all other Poultry Wares that shall be sold or offered to be sold or be in the Shops or other place or places of Sale of all and every or any other person or persons whatsoever being ffree of the said City and of all other persons useing and exerciseing the Art Trade or Mistery of a Poulter or of selling Eggs Butter or Coneys Poultry Wares within the said City of London Suburbs or Liberties thereof or within the space of 7 Miles of the same City or in any market or other place within the said City of London Suburbs or Liberties of the same or within 7 Miles of the same and if upon their search or otherwise they shall find that any of the persons aforesaid hath sold or offered to put to sale any defective stinking or unwholesome Poultry Wares Butter Eggs or Coneys That then the Master Wardens and Assistants of the said Company for the time being or any four of them whereof the Master and one of the Wardens of the said Company for the time being to be two shall and doe forthwith make complaint thereof to and seize the said stinking defective and unwholesome wares and carry the same to or before some or one of the Justices of the Peace of the City of London or to or before some or one Justice of the peace of any other County City Liberty or Precinct within 7 Miles of the said City of London to the intent that the same Wares may be disposed of according to the Laudable Custome of the City of London touching unwholesome Victualls and to the intent that the said person or persons selling and uttering or offering to sell or utter the same may be prosecuted and proceeded against according to the Law but if any of the said person or persons aforesaid shall refuse to permit and suffer the said Master Wardens and Assistants of the said Company for the time being or any ffour of them whereof the Master and one of the Wardens of the said Company for the time being to be Two to search try and examine his or their Poultry Wares Eggs Butter or Coneys to see whether they are good sweet and wholesome for Mans body or noe and for that End to enter into his Shop or other place or places of Sale or place or places where his or their Poultry Wares Eggs Butter or Coneys shall then be that then every such person and persons so refuseing shall for every such offence or refuseall forfeit and pay unto the Master Wardens and Assistants of the said Company for the time being to and for the use of the said Company the sume of Fforty shillings of good and lawfull money of England

20 Item That no person or persons now Inhabiting and dwelling or that hereafter shall Inhabit or dwell within the said City of London or within 7 Miles of the same City and there use and exercise the said Art or Mistery nor any other person being ffree of the said Company shall hereafter take any person or persons not being borne within their Majesties obeisance or dominions to be his or their apprentice or apprentices or by any colour or device knowingly sett to work any Man's apprentice neither shall retaine keep or sett to work in the said Art or Mistery any person or persons other than his own children that had or have not served as an apprentice or apprentices to the said Trade or Mistery by the space of 7 years above the space of one month before he shall take and bind him by Indenture to be made by the Clerk of the said Company for the time being to be his apprentice for the terme of 7 years at the least and that

every person that offendeth in any point of this ordinance shall forfeit and pay to the Master Wardens and Assistants of the said Company for the time being to and for the use of the said Company for every such offence the sume of Fforty shillings of lawfull money of England

21 **Item** That the Clerk of the said Company for the time being and none else shall have the writing and ingrossing of all Indentures for apprentices that shall be bound to any ffreeman or woman or other person or persons being members and ffree of the said Company that now doe or doth inhabit or dwell or that hereafter shall inhabit or dwell within the said City of London Suburbs or Liberties thereof or within 7 Miles of the same City and there use and exercise the said Art or Mistery and that the Clerke of the said Company for the time being shall and may take for his ffee and pains for the writing and Ingrossing of every such pair of Indentures if the said apprentice shall be bound in open Court Three shillings and sixpence of lawfull money of England And that the Apprentices so bound in open Court shall pay to the Master Wardens and Assistants of the said Company for the time being to and for the use of the said Company Two shillings and sixpence of lawfull money of England and to the Beadle of the said Company One shilling and if the said Apprentice or Apprentices shall be bound out of Court then he and they shall pay unto the Clerke of the said Company for the time being for the Indentures of Apprenticeship the sume of Seven shillings of lawfull money of England And also to the Master Wardens and Assistants of the said Company for the time being to and for the use of the said Company the sume of Ffive shillings of like lawfull money and to the Beadle or Beadles of the said Company for the time being Two shillings of like lawfull money And to the Clerk of the said Company for the entry of the presentment eight pence And if any of the said persons taking

Apprentices as aforesaid shall make or cause to be made any Indentures contrary to the effect purport and true meaning of this present Ordinance that then every person so doeing shall forfeit and pay to the Master Wardens and Assistants of the said Company for the time being to and for the use of the said Company the sume of Fforty shillings of Lawfull money of England to be distributed and divided in manner and forme following that is to say Thirteen shillings and four pence thereof to the Clerke of the said Company for the time being and Three shillings and four pence other part thereof to the Beadle or Beadles of the said Company for the time being and the residue thereof to the use of the said Company And if the said Clerk for the time being shall neglect to make true entryes of the said presentments of every or any such apprentice or apprentices or of their being bound as aforesaid that then for every such neglect and default the clerk of the said Company for the time being making such default shall forfeit and pay to the Master Wardens and Assistants of the said Company for the time being to and for the use of the said Company the sume of six shillings and eight pence of like lawfull money of England

22 **Item** For as much as it is found by experience that the neglect of Inrolling of apprentices according to the custome of the City of London and the oath of a ffreeman within the ffirst year of their terme doth give great liberty to apprentices to discharge and ffree themselves from their Masters service and to goe at large to the ruine of many a youth whose ffriends by binding him otherwise intended for prevention whereof It is ordered that every person being a ffreeman of the City of London and a member of the said Company shall within one yeare next after any apprentice shall be bound to him cause the said apprentice to be enrolled according to the antient and laudable custome of the City of London and

if he shall faile or neglect to doe the same That then he shall forfeit and pay to the Master Wardens and Assistants of the said Company for the time being to and for the use of the said Company for every such offence or neglect the sume of six shillings eight pence of lawfull money of England

23 Item For preventing all abuses in putting away or assigneing or setting over of apprentices It is ordered and established that noe person or persons now inhabiting or dwelling or that hereafter shall inhabit or dwell within the said City of London Liberties or suburbs thereof or within seven miles of the same City and there use and exercise the said Art or Mistery being members and ffree of the said Company whether ffree of the City of London or noe shall at any time hereafter Bargaine sell give grant assigne or set over or otherwise dispose of or put away any apprentice or apprentices to him bound or before to him assigned or set over willingly suffer any such apprentice or apprentices to depart out of his or their service without the consent order and approbation of the Master Wardens and Assistants of the said Company for the time being or the more part of them whereof the Master of the said Company for the time being to be one And that every Master to whom such Apprentice or Apprentices shall be set over shall pay to the Master Wardens and Assistants of the said Company for the time being To and for the use of the said Company Two shillings and to the Clerk of the said Company for the time being for entering the same one shilling And for endorseing the same on the Indenture of apprenticeship six pence and to the Beadle of the said Company six pence of lawfull money of England And that every person that doth contrary to this order shall for every such his offence forfeit and pay to the Master Wardens and Assistants of the said Company for the time being To and for the use of the said Company Twenty shillings of lawfull money of England.

THE WORSHIPFUL COMPANY OF POULTERS. 39

24 **Item** That every apprentice to any of the said Company within three months next after the years of his Apprenticeship shall be ended if he have well and truely served and not deserved the contrary shall offer himself to the Master and Wardens of the said Company for the time being to be made ffree of the same Company or else he shall forfeit and pay to the Master Wardens and Assistants of the said Company for the time being To and for the use of the said Company for not offering himself within the said three months to be made ffree of the said Company the sume of thirteen shillings and ffour pence of lawfull money of England and for every month afterwards that he continueth without making such offer two shillings and six pence of lawfull money of England **Provided** always And it is hereby ordained that if the default of the not making ffree of any such apprentice shall be adjudged by the Master Wardens and Assistants of the said Company for the time being or by the more part of them to be in the Master or Mistress of any such apprentice that then the said Master or Mistress shall pay the aforesaid ffines and the apprentice thereof to be quit but if default thereof be adjudged in the apprentice to pay the same ffines himselfe

25 **Item** That every person or persons that hereafter shall be made ffree of the said Company shall pay to the Master Wardens and Assistants of the said Company for the time being to and for the use of the said Company at the time of his being made ffree of the said Company the sume of Two shillings and six pence of good and lawfull money of England and to the Clerke of the said Company for the time being for entering his admission to the ffreedom of the said Company three shillings and six pence and to each of the Beadles of the said Company for the time being twelve pence And also shall as is usual and hath been for a long time accustomed in the said

Company ffreely give to the Master Wardens and Assistants of the said Company to and for the use of the said Company one silver spoone of the value of thirteen shillings and four pence as a present or in lieu thereof thirteen shillings and four pence in money and that every person and persons hereafter to be made free shall before the Master and Wardens of the same Mistery for the time being be sworne and take the oath of a freeman of the said Company which oath is hereafter mentioned and expressed

26 **Item** That noe person or persons now being or that hereafter shall be free of the City of London and of the said Company and that now use or hereafter shall use or exercise the said art or Mistery or any thing thereunto belonging within the said City Liberties or Suburbs thereof or within seven miles of the said City shall at any time or times hereafter retaine hire or take into service or any other way set to work in the said Art or Mistery any Alien or stranger borne out of their Majestyes obeisance nor any foreigner whatsoever nor any other person or persons but only ffreemen of the said City and of the said Art or Mistery or their own children or apprentices which shall be bound to the same Art or Mistery And that whosoever offendeth in any part of this Ordinance shall forfeit and pay unto the Master Wardens and Assistants of the said Company for the time being To and for the use of the said Company for every such offence Twenty shillings and for every week after that he continueth any such offence Six shillings and eight pence of good and lawfull money of England

27 **Item** It is ordered that every person ffree of the said Company or Member of that body That useth or that hereafter shall use or exercise the Art or Mistery of a Poulter within the said City of London or

Libertyes or Surburbs thereof or within seven miles of the same City shall at all times hereafter be and shew themselves to be of a good and honest behaviour and bearing as well in their words as in their actions towards the Master Wardens and Assistants of the said Company for the time being and be Tractable conformable and obedient to all and every the lawfull constitutions Orders Ordinances and Institutions made or to be made by the Master Wardens and Assistants of the said Company for the time being and if any such person or persons now useing or exerciseing or that hereafter shall use or exercise the said Art or Mistery within the City of London Liberties or Surburbs thereof or within 7 miles of the said City shall at any time or times hereafter be found disobedient to the Master Wardens and Assistants of the said Company for the time being or any of them in any of the matters and things of the Common Concerne of the said Company or the Government thereof or in the due execution of these presents ordinances and constitutions or any of them to the Lett hindrance or disturbance of the due execution of any their offices or of anything touching the same or do or take upon him or them to make any private assembly or secret meeting or attempts against the Master Wardens and Assistants of the said Company for the time being for or to the Violation or Breach of any ordinance order or constitution now or heretofore had or to be had made ordained or constituted by the Master Wardens and Assistants of the said Company for the time being for the good Rule and Governement of the same Company or the exercise of the said Art or Mistery and of all persons useing or exerciseing the same or doe unjustly or wrongfully practice or attempt any thing which in anywise may be Slandrous or hurtfull to the Master Wardens and Assistants of the said Company for the time being or to any of them in relation to their said offices or shall at any time hereafter privately or openly revile or misuse with any evil or undecent speeches or words of reproach the Master Wardens and Assistants of the said Company for the time being or any of them or shall openly or privately revile misuse or abuse with any evil or undecent speeches or words of Reproach or beat or strike any other person or persons then being a ffreeman or member of the said Company that then every person offending or doing contrary to any part of this Ordinance shall forfeit and pay to the Master Wardens and Assistants of the said Company for the time being to and for the use of the said Company for every time soe offending or doeing the sume of ffive shillings of lawfull money of England

28 Item That every person who shall at any time hereafter be made free of the City of London and of the said Company by ffine or purchase shall before he be admitted accepted received and sworne pay to the Master Wardens and Assistants of the said Company for the time being to and for the use of the said Company such sume and sumes of money as apprentices bound to any of the said Company of the said Art or Mistery of a Poulter usually do or ought to pay for their admission to the ffreedome of the said Company And shall also pay unto the Master Wardens and Assistants of the said Company for the time being to and for the use of the said Company the sume of Twenty pounds more of good and lawful money of England at the least or such bigger or greater sume of money as the Master Wardens and Assistants of the said Company for the time being or the more part of them whereof the Master and one of the Wardens of the said Company for the time being to be two shall think fitt require or demand and to the Clerk of the said Company for the time being for entring his admission to the Ffreedome of the said Company the sume of seven shillings

29 Item It is ordered and ordained that noe Leases demises

Annuities Grants or Gifts of what nature or kind whatsoever of any house or houses Lands Tenements or other things whatsoever appertaining or belonging to the Company aforesaid or any obligations Bills or Specialties for any sume or sumes of money shall pass under the Comon Seale of this Corporation or Society unless the same be ordered soe by the Master Wardens and Assistants of the said Company for the time being or the more part of them whereof the Master and one of the Wardens of the said Company to be two at a Court by them to be holden upon paine that every one of the Master and Wardens of the said Company for the time being under whose Custody or charge the said Common Seale then shall be remaining for every such act shall forfeit and pay to the Master Wardens and Assistants of the said Company for the time being to and for the use of the said Company the sume of One hundred pounds apiece and that when and as often as any such case shall happen

30 **Item** that noe person or persons now useing or exerciseing or that hereafter shall use or exercise the said Art or Mistery of a Poulter or anything thereunto appertaining and that now doe or doth inhabit or dwell or that hereafter shall inhabit or dwell within the said City of London Suburbs or Liberties thereof or within seven miles of the same City shall at any time or times hereafter intice persuade receive or take in his her or their service or house any man or woman apprentice Covenant Servant or Journeyman of the same art or Mistery untill the time of every such apprentice covenant Servant or Journeyman be ended and he she or they shall be cleared of his her or their Master Mistresses or Dames Service and Debt unless it be otherwise ordered by the Master Wardens and Assistants of the said Company for the time being or the more part of them whereof the Master and one of the Wardens of the said Company for the time being to be two And that every person that doth contrary to this

ordinance or any part thereof shall forfeit and pay to the Master Wardens and Assistants of the said Company for the time being To and for the use of the said Company for every such offence or doeing contrary to this ordinance the sume of Twenty shillings of lawfull money of England

31 **Item** It is ordered that if any person or persons useing or that hereafter shall use or exercise the Art or Mistery of Poulters within the City of London Liberties or Suburbs thereof or within seven miles compass of the same shall at any time or times hereafter conspire covenant promise or make any oaths agreements or undertakings not to sell their victualls but at certain prices or not to sell the same under certain prices or any other covenant promise oath agreement or undertakeings whatsoever whereby or by means whereof the prices of such Poultry Wares Butter Eggs Coneys or Victualls may be either inhansed raised or kept up that then every person soe conspireing covenanting promiseing or offending shall forfeit and pay to the Master Wardens and Assistants of the said Company for the time being to and for the use of the said Company for every such offence the sume of Ffive pounds of good and lawfull money of England

32 **Item** For as much as forestalling is an injurious thing to the Common wealth and therefore by the Laws and Statutes of this Realme is prohibited and forbidden and yet notwithstanding by some evil disposed persons much used It is therefore ordered that no person or persons now being or which hereafter shall be free of the said Company or any other person or persons now useing or exerciseing or that hereafter shall use or exercise the said Art or Mistery or that now doth or doe or hereafter shall inhabit or dwell within the said City of London Surburbs or Liberties thereof or within 7 miles of the same City nor any of his her or

their Ffactor or Ffactors Servant or Servants nor any other person or persons by his her or their order direction or procurement shall at any time or times hereafter Goe or ride to any place or places being within twenty miles of the said City of London with intent or purpose to meet or buy any Poultery wares butter or eggs being brought upon the Roads towards the said City of London of intent and purpose to be sold nor shall directly or indirectly make any manner of price contract covenant or Bargaine for any such Poultry Wares Butter Eggs or Coneys before the same shall be brought into some open Markett in the said City of London Surburbs or Liberties thereof to be sold nor shall Buy Contract covenant or Bargaine for any such Poultry Wares Butter or Eggs brought to any of the said Marketts to be sold but in open Markett upon pain that every person or persons offending or doing contrary to this ordinance or any part thereof shall forfeit and pay to the Master Wardens and Assistants of the said Company for the time being to and for the use of the said Company for every such offence the sume of Ffive pounds of Lawfull money of England

33 Item That every person that now is or hereafter shall be ffree of the said Company or member thereof and shall use or exercise the said Art or Mistery within the said City of London Suburbs or Liberties thereof or within seven miles of the said City and all and every person and persons which now doe or shall hereafter use or exercise the trade of a Poulter or sell any Poultry Wares Butter Eggs and Coneys or any of them within the said City of London Suburbs or Liberties thereof or within seven miles of the same City shall from time to time and at all times hereafter during all the time he shall use or exercise the said Art or Mistery or sell Poultry Wares Butter Eggs and Coneys or any of them as aforesaid have and use at his and her own choice and election either a

shop or one constant place of sale and no more for the vending and selling of Poultry Wares Butter Eggs and Coneys within the said City of London Suburbs or Liberties thereof or within seven miles of the same City And that every one of the said persons who hath not or shall not have a shop but shall have and use another place of sale for the purposes aforesaid shall give notice unto the Master and Wardens of the said Company for the time being of such his other constant place of sale and where the same now is or hereafter shall be and that none of the persons aforesaid shall at any time hereafter either by him or herselfe or by his or her servant or Servants Agent or Agents or by any other person or persons for his or her use or by or with his or her consent or appointment either directly or indirectly have keepe occupy or use any more than one shop or one place of sale for vending selling or uttering of Poultry Wares Butter Eggs and Coneys or any of them within the said City of London Suburbs or Liberties thereof or within seven Miles of the same City upon paine that every person and persons soe offending in any of the particulars aforesaid in this Ordinance expressed or doeing contrary to the true intent and meaning of this ordinance or any part thereof shall forfeit and pay to the Master Wardens and Assistants of the said Company for the time being to and for the use of the said Company for every such offence the sume of Ffive pounds of lawfull English money

34 **Item** That noe person of the Livery of the said Company shall from henceforth have or keep above two apprentices at one time and none of the Yeomanry shall have or keep above one upon paine to forfeit and pay to the Master Wardens and Assistants of the said Company for the time being To and for the use of the said Company for the ffirst offence or Breach of this order the sume of Ffive pounds and for every six months afterwards that he shall continue the said offence or Breach thereof forty

shillings of lawful money of England Provided always that it shall be lawfull to and for every such person always within the space of one year next before the expiration of the Terme of apprenticeship of his then apprentice to take and have one other apprentice to succeed that apprentice whose apprenticeship is to expire at that years end

35 Item It is ordered ordained and established that noe matter or thing order decree or Judgment which doth or shall concerne the Generall Estate or Common profit of the said Company shall be had made done passed or ordered but in the presence of the Master and Wardens of the said Company for the time being or of such Deputy or Deputyes as in case of his or their absence at any Courts or other Assembly of the said Company shall according to the true meaning of these ordinances be deputed or appointed to act in his or their place or places or the Major part of them And that the vote assent or agreement of the Major part of them so assembled and present in any Court of Assistance shall be sufficient and availeable for touching or concerning any matter or thing so to be by them had made ordered passed or done to bind and conclude the said Company and every or any member thereof

36 Item It is ordained and established that noe person or persons shall carry or cause to be carried any Poultry Wares Butter Eggs or Coneys about the Streets Lanes or By places within the City of London Suburbs or Liberties of the same by way of hawkeing or offering to sale to any person or persons within the said City of London Suburbs and Liberties of the same out of the Publique Marketts or any of them contrary to the antient custome of the said City of London upon paine that every person and persons that offend

against the true meaning of this Ordinance shall forfeit and pay to the Master Wardens and Assistants of the said Company for the time being to and for the use of the said Company for every such offence the sume of fforty shillings of lawfull money of England

37 Item That for the preventing the Inhansing the price of Dead Poultry Wares that shall at any time hereafter be brought to the said City of London Suburbs or Liberties thereof It is ordained and established that noe Porter nor other person or persons whatever but the proper owner of the said dead Poultry Wares or his or their Meniall Servant or Servants actually and bona fide liveing with him or her in his or her dwelling house and being in his or her service shall sell any such Poultry Wares neither shall any Porter or other person or persons whatsoever either in the Markett or in any place out of the Markett informe any person or persons who have or hath brought any such Dead Poultry Wares or shall be bringing or on the way to bring any such dead Poultry Wares into the said City Liberties or Suburbs thereof or into any Markett within the said City Suburbs or Liberties thereof with intent to sell the same again what the prices of Dead Poultry Wares then are at or shall be upon paine that every person and persons offending in the premises contrary to the true intent and meaning of this ordinance shall forfeit and pay to the Master Wardens and Assistants of the said Company for the time being to and for the use of the said Company for every such offence the sume of fforty shillings of good and lawfull money of England.

38 Item That every person that shall hereafter be made ffree of the said Company not being before ffree of the said City of

London shall within three months next after his being admitted to the ffreedome or being made ffree of the said Company procure him or herselfe to be made ffree and to be admitted to the ffreedome of the said City upon paine to forfeit and pay to the Master Wardens and Assistants of the said Company for the time being To and for the use of the said Company for the ffirst offence in not being made ffree of the said City before the end of the said three months the sume of Three pounds of good and lawfull money of England and for every month after that he shall continue unadmitted ffree of the said City the sume of Twenty shillings of lawfull money of England

39 **Item** For that by experience it hath been found That Poulters and others using the Art or Mistery of Poulters and selling Poultery Wares Buying and contracting for or taking Leases of Warrens of Coneys and Decoys of Wild Ffowle hath been a great occasion not only of Inhansing prices of Coneys and Wild Ffowle but also divers times of the selling stinking defective and unwholsome Coneys and Wild Ffowle in regard among other reasons that at certain seasons those Poulters are overflocked with Coneys and Wild Ffowle more than they can sell or utter whilst the said Coneys and Wild Ffowle are good and wholesome for Mans body for the preventing and avoiding of such abuses for the future It is ordained and established that noe ffree man or ffreewoman of the said Company nor any other person or persons useing or exerciseing or which hereafter shall use or exercise the said Art or Mistery of a Poulter or selling of Poultery Wares within the City of London Suburbs or Liberties thereof or within seven miles of the same shall at any time hereafter without the consent of the Master Wardens and Assistants

of the said Company for the time being or the Major part of them whereof the Master and one of the Wardens of the said Company to be two by any Art means craft devise or covin whatever either by him or hereselfe or by any other person or persons by his her or their order direction or appointment or in trust for him her or them Buy Bargaine or Contract for or take any Lease of any Warren of Coneys or Decoy of Wild Ffowle or buy bargaine or contract for with the Owners Ffarmers or Proprietors of any Warren of Coneys or Decoys of Wild Fowle or with their or any of their Servant or Servants or with any other on their or any of their behalfs or in trust for them or any of them for the Coneys or Wild Fowle taken or to be taken in or proceeding or comeing from any Warren of Coneys or Decoy of Wild Fowle or shall have receive and take into his her or their custody Ingrosse or by way of wholesale any Coneys or any Wild Fowle to wit Duck Mallard Teale or Widgeon upon paine that every one offending herein or doeing contrary to the Tenor true intent and meaning of this ordinance shall forfeit and pay unto the Master Wardens and Assistants of the said Company for the time being To and for the use of the said Company for the ffirst offence the sume of Ffive pounds of good and lawfull money of England and for every week after wherein he she or they shall continue to sell Coneys or Wild Fowle soe contracted for bought or received as aforesaid contrary to the true intent and meaning of this ordinance the sume of Twenty shillings of good and lawfull money of England it being intended that to prevent all abuses in the Buying and ingrossing of Poultry Wares the Master Wardens and Assistants of the said Company or such persons as they shall depute shall only by the same Comodities and the same when bought for the Companys use shall at reasonable rates be disposed to and amongst the respective members of the said

Company and in such proportions as shall be agreed hereafter by a Court of Assistants

40 **Item** That no ffreeman or ffreewoman of the said Company nor any other person or persons that now doth or doe or hereafter shall use or exercise the Art or Mistery of a Poulter or doth or doe hereafter shall sell any Poultry Wares within the said City of London Liberties or Suburbs thereof or within Seven Miles of the same City shall at any time or times hereafter Buy Bargaine or Contract for or get into their hands any Coneys or any Wild Fowle to wit Duck Mallard Teal or Widgeon or any of them that shall be brought to any Markett within the said City Liberties or Suburbs thereof to be sold with intent to sell the same again within the said City Liberties or Suburbs thereof or within seven miles of the same City upon paine to forfeit to the Master Wardens and Assistants of the said Company for the time being To and for the use of the said Company for every such offence the sume of Tenn shillings of good and lawfull money of England

41 **Item** That noe person using or exerciseing or which hereafter shall use or exercise the Art or Mistery of a Poulter or shall sell or put to sale or offer to sell or put to sale any Poultry Wares Eggs Butter or Coneys within the said City Suburbs or Liberties thereof or within seven Miles of the said City shall sell in any of the Marketts within the said City Liberties or Suburbs thereof or within seven miles of the said City upon By days or any other days than such as are or shall be Publique and Common Markett Days upon paine to forfeit and pay to the Master Wardens and Assistants of the said Company for the time being to and for the use of the

said Company for every such offence the sume of Tenn shillings of good snd lawfull money of England

42 **Item** That every ffreeman and ffreewoman of the said Company and everyone useing or exerciseing or which hereafter shall use or exercise the said Art or Mistery of a Poulter or shall sell Poultry Wares Butter Eggs or Coneys within the said City Suburbs or Liberties thereof or within seven miles of the same City shall upon every of the said Quarter days or ffeasts of St. Michael the Archangell the Birth of our Lord Christ the Annunciation of the Blessed Virgin Mary and the Nativity of St. John the Baptist or upon such day within twenty days next after every of the said Quarterdays or ffeasts as by the Master and Wardens of the said Company for the time being shall for sueh purpose be appointed bring or send his or her Quarteridge To wit six pence a quarter to the Common Hall of the said Company or such place as the Master and Wardens of the said Company for the time being or the Major part of them whereof the Master of the said Company for the time being to be one shall for that purpose appoint and there pay the same to the Master Wardens and Assistants of the said Company for the time being upon pain to forfeit and pay to the Master Wardens and Assistants of the said Company for the time being to and for the use of the said Company for every such offence or neglect the sume of Fforty shillings of good and lawfull money of England

43 **Item** It is ordered that all and every sume and sumes of money whatsoever which by the Master Wardens and Assistants of the said Company for the time being or any of them shall be received of any person or persons whatsoever for any ffine or ffines or otherwise by force

of any Order or Ordinance aforesaid shall be Imployed and Bestowed To the use and Supportation of the said Company and for the defraying of the charges costs and expenses of the Master Wardens and Assistants of the said Company for the time being in and about the business and affairs of the said Company and for noe other use or uses whatsoever

44 Item It is by the Master Wardens and Assistants of the said Company ordered ordained and established that all and every the penalties and forfeitures Sume and Sumes of money to be incurred or forfeited by vertue or means of the ordinances aforesaid or any of them shall be recovered by action of Debt Bill or Plaint to be commenced brought or prosecuted in the name of the Master Wardens and Assistants of Poulters London or in such name or names as shall be advised or thought fitt in any of their Majesties Courts of Record at Westminster in the County of Middlesex or for offences committed in London either in their Majesties said Courts of Record at Westminster aforesaid or in any of the Courts of Record holden within the City of London or elsewhere and that the Master Wardens and Assistants of the said Company for the time being or those in whose names such action or actions shall be brought shall in all and every such suite to be commenced and prosecuted by vertue of the aforesaid ordinances or any of them against any offender or offenders against the said ordinances or any of them recover the ordinary costs of suite to be expended in or about the prosecution thereof

THE OATH OF A MASTER

Now that you are elected and chosen to be Master of the Art or Mistery of Poulters of the City of London you shall so long as you continue Master justly truely and diligently according to the best of your skill and cunning execute your said office and that with Indifferency in every respect and also to the utmost of your power and skill you shall endeavour to put in due execution all the good and lawfull ordinances made or to be made touching the said Mistery without assessing or punishing any person for Envy hatred or malice, or spareing any person for reward meed dread favour or affection and of all and every such goods plate jewells money and other things that by reason of your said office shall come to your hands possession or custody you shall make a good true and plaine and perfect account to the Master Wardens and Assistants of the said Mistery for the time being according to the ordinances in that case made and provided Soe helpe you God

THE OATH OF A WARDEN

Now that you are elected and chosen to be Warden of the Art or Mistery of the Poulters of the City of London you shall so long as you continue Warden Justly truely and diligently according to the best of your skill and cunning execute your said office and that with Indifferency in every respect and also to the utmost of your power and skill you shall endeavour to put in due execution all the good and lawfull ordinances made or to be made touching the said Mistery without assessing or punishing any person for Envy hatred or Malice or spareing any person for reward meed dread favour or affection and of all and every such goods plate Jewells money and all other things that by reason of your said office shall come to your hands possession or custody you shall make a good true plaine and perfect account to the Master Wardens and assistants of the said Mistery for the time being according to the ordinances in that case made and provided   Soe helpe you God

THE OATH OF THE ASSISTANTS

Now that you are elected and chosen to be Assistant to the Master and Wardens of the Art or Mistery of Poulters of the City of London you shall so long as you continue to them an Assistant give your diligence and be ready to assist the said Master and Wardens when and as often as you shall be called thereunto haveing noe lawfull lett or leave to the contrary and shall to best of your skill and cunning so near as you can with all Indifferency give your best and soundest advice opinion and Counsell to the said Master and Wardens in all such things as they shall lawfully require your advice opinion and Counsel in or touching the said art or Mistery or touching any the orders or ordinances made or to be made concerning the said Mistery or any person useing the same or being ffree thereof you shall not in giving your advice opinion or counsel spare any person for meed dread favour or affection or assess or punish any person for Envy hatred or Malice but shall uprightly and justly give your advice according to the truth soe neare as you can   Soe helpe you God

THE OATH of HIM WHO WILL DISCHARGE HIMSELF OF THE LIVERY

You shall swear that the just debts which you now owe and intend to pay being paid you are not worth in reall and personall Estate the Sume of One hundred and ffifty Marks   Soe helpe you God

THE OATH OF A FFREEMAN

You shall swear you shall be true and faithfull to our Sovereigne Lord and Lady William and Mary King and Queene of England you shall be obedient at all times hereafter in all matters lawfull to the Master and Wardens of the Art and Mistery of Poulters London and to their Successors for the time being you shall not withstand or disobey the Summons of the Master and Wardens of the said Mistery for the time being by their officer therefore assigned without you have a lawfull and reasonable excuse And for your owne part you shall well and truely observe performe fulfill and keep all and singular the lawfull and reasonable Orders and Ordinances made and to be made by the said Master and Wardens and Assistants of the said Mistery for the Good Rule and Government of them and their Successors and shall not doe anything to the damage prejudice or rebuke of the said Master Wardens Assistants and Commonalty but in these things and in all other things you shall doe use and behave yourselfe as a good Citizen of the City of London and a Ffreeman of the said Company ought to doe Soe helpe you God

THE OATH OF A CLERKE

Now that you are elected and chosen to be Clerke to the Master Wardens and Assistants of the Art or Mistery of the Poulters London You shall soe long as you continue their Clerke be willing and ready haveing noe leave or lawfull lett to the contrary to attend the said Master and Wardens when they shall require you for the business of your place as their clerke and shall endeavour yourselfe to make true entries of all things belonging to your office committed to your charge without all partiality for favour affection Lucre gaine hatred or malice you shall not willingly commit or doe any thing to the prejudice hurt or damage of the Master Wardens and Assistants of the said Mistery of Poulters London but well and truely you shall execute your said office so near as you can as a good and lawfull Clerke ought to doe Soe helpe you God

THE OATH OF A BEADLE.

Now that you are elected and chosen Beadle to the Master Wardens and Assistants of the Art or Mistery of the Poulters London you shall so long as you continue their Beadle Summon all and every such person and persons as the said Master and Wardens or any of them shall at any time command to be summoned according to the ordinances in that case made and provided without spareing of any persons for ffavour affection Lucre gaine hatred or malice you shall endeavour yourselfe as near as you can at all times to doe and execute the lawfull commandments of the said Master Wardens and Assistants and belonging to your office you shall not wittingly or willingly commit or doe any thing to the prejudice damage hurt or rebuke of the said Master Wardens and Assistants but diligently well and truly you shall execute your office as near as you can as a good Beadle ought to doe   Soe helpe you God.

In witnesse whereof the Master Wardens and the more part of the said Company have subscribed their names hereunto and have caused the

Common Seale of the said Company to be affixed hereunto the day and yeare first above written

NATHANIEL BALDICK *Master*	EDWARD DRAPER	R. JOHNSON
JOHN ARCHER } *Wardens*	JOHN WIBIRD	THO PEWSEY
RICHARD WALKDEN }	HENRY KINDON	RICH^D PYKE
	PHILIP LEMON	HENRY NEWDICK
JOHN BISSELL	THOMAS CARTER	EDMOND OKELY
JOHN WILKES	THOMAS CLARKE	JOHN LOCKYER
AMBROSE SHIPWASH	JOHN HEWETT	JOHN WHIFFIN
WILLIAM OLIVER	JONATHAN BROWNE	

𝕸𝖊𝖒𝖔𝖗𝖆𝖓𝖉 that the orders ordinances and constitutions above mentioned were according to the Statute in that case made and provided examined and approved of by the Right Honourable Sir John Somers Knight Lord keeper of the great seal of England The Right Honourable Sir John Holt Knight Lord Chief Justice of their Majesties Court of Kings Bench at Westminster in the County of Middlesex and by the Right Honourable Sir George Treby Knight Lord Chief Justice of their Majesties Court of Common Pleas at Westminster aforesaid and they doe hereby approve of the same 𝕴𝖓 𝖜𝖎𝖙𝖓𝖊𝖘𝖘 whereof the said Lord Keeper Lord Chief Justice of their Majesties Court of Kings Bench and Lord Chief Justice of their Majesties said Court of Common Pleas the eighteenth day of Aprill in the fifth year of the reigne of Our Sovereign Lord and Lady William and Mary by the Grace of God of England Scotland Ffrance and Ireland King

and Queen Defenders of the ffaith etc   Annoq; Domini One Thousand
six hundred ninety-three

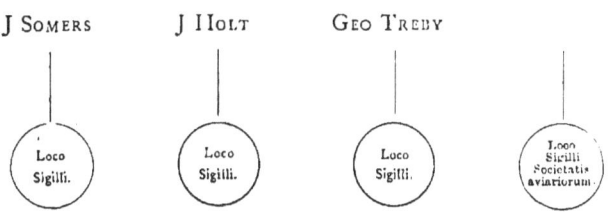

𝔄 𝕿𝖆𝖇𝖑𝖊 expressing the Orders in this Book of Ordinances
contained with their number and of every leaf wherein
they are to be found

𝕴𝖒𝖕𝖗𝖎𝖒𝖎𝖘 the Statute of King William and Queen Mary recited

ORDINANCES

		PAGE
1	The Election day .	16
2	The Election of Master . .	16
3	The Election of the Wardens . .	17
4	Ffor swearing the Master and Wardens .	18
5	Ffor Election of Assistants	18
6	Penalty for elected Master Wardens and Assistants refusing their respective offices or omitting taking their respective Oaths	20
7	Assistants to appear in their Livery Gowns on Election day	21
8	The Election of Liverymen .	22

E

		PAGE
9	The Master and Wardens to Sitt in their Courts in Gowns and the Livery attending the Court to come in their Gowns	24
10	The Election of Renter Warden . .	24
11	To prevent Selling the Companys Lands .	26
12	The Election of a Clerke	27
13	The Election of Beadles	28
14	Ffor keeping Two half yearly Courts their Power and the Penalty for not obeying their Summonses . . .	29
15	Ffor keeping Courts of Assistants the power of such Courts and of Election of a new Master if the Master for the time being neglect to call such Court . .	30
16	None to be absent at any Court without License unless the Master and Wardens licensing be then present and pay the ffine and Quarteridge due from the person so licensed	32
17	The Master not attending said Courts by reason of Sickness the Major part of the Assistants may choose a Master pro hac Vice	32
18	Ffor payment of Quarteridge . .	33
19	To search and oversee Poultry Wares	33
20	None to take an apprentice not born within the King's Obeysance Imploy a Fforeigner or keep a designed apprentice at work above a month before binding the Clerk to make the Indentures.	35
21	The Clerks ffees setled upon making apprentices Indentures with penalty on such as gett them made elsewhere	36
22	Ffor Inrolling Apprentices	37

		PAGE
23	None to turn over his apprentice without the consent of the Company.	38
24	Every apprentice to offer himself to be made ffree within three months after the expiration of his apprenticeship.	39
25	The ffees upon a Ffreedom setled and an appointment of an oath.	39
26	None to sett any Fforeigner or Alien to work	40
27	To be of good behaviour in words and actions with penalty	40
28	Ffine for being made ffree by Redemption	42
29	No leases &c to pass under the Common Seal unless by order of Court	42
30	None to take into his Service anothers apprentice servant &c without an order of Court with Penalty	43
31	Ffine for conspiracies relating to the Sale of Poultry Wares	44
32	To prevent fforestalling.	44
33	Persons to have but one place of sale	45
34	The Livery to keep but two apprentices at one time and the Yeomanry but one.	46
35	No order &c concerning the Common Estate of the Company shall be made but in the presence of the Master Wardens and Assistants.	47
36	None to carry any Poultry Wares into the Street or by way of Hawking.	47
37	Ffor prevention of Enhancing the prices of dead Poultry Wares.	48
38	Persons made ffree of the said Company to procure their ffreedom of the City of London within three months	48
39	None to take by Lease any Coney Warren or Decoy of Wild Fowl	49

		PAGE
40	None to buy any Poultry Wares in Open Markett with design to sell them again	51
41	None to sell in Marketts upon by days . . .	51
42	Ffor payment of Quarteridge	52
43	All ffines and other profits to be imployed to the use of the Company	52
44	Ffor the Recovery of all Fforfeitures and Penalties . .	53
	The oath of a Master . .	53
	The oath of a Warden	54
	The oath of the Assistants	55
	The oath of him who will discharge himself of the Livery .	55
	The oath of a Ffreeman	56
	The oath of a Clerke	56
	The oath of a Beadle .	57

BECKFORD MAYOR

A Common Councel holden in the Chamber of the Guildhall of the City of London on Wednesday the twenty sixth day of October 1763

This Day the Committee having pursuant to the order of this Court of the eleventh instant filled up the blanks in the Bill for regulating the Company of Poulters London did deliver the same so filled up into this Court and the same was read a third time and a Motion was made and Question put that the Bill as now read do pass into a Law and become the **Act** of this Court **It** was resolved in the Affirmative and ordered accordingly which **Act** follows in these words

An Act for regulating the Company of Poulters of London

Whereas the ffellowship Company of Poulters London are and have been an Antient ffellowship Company and have been long since incorporated by the name of the Master Wardens and Assistants of Poulters London and have obtained several Royal Grants for Confirmation of their privileges **And** by their Constitutions the said Master Wardens and Assistants ought to have the View oversight Search and Correction of all persons whatsoever of the said Company and of the Wares Goods and Commoditys by them sold or offered to sale and to punish and correct offences deceipts abuses or Misdemeanors in the occupation of the said trade of Poulter

And whereas many persons who exercise the Trade of Poulter within the City of London have obtained their ffreedoms of other Companys by Redemption and otherwise by reason whereof the said Company of Poulters is much diminished and may fall into decay and such persons suing the said Trade can not be regularly searched nor the deceits and Misdemeanors in the said Trade properly corrected **For remedy whereof be it enacted ordained and established** By the Right Honorable the Lord Mayor Aldermen and Commons of the City of London in this present Common councel Assembled and by the authority of the same that from and after the Twenty fifth day of December One thousand seven hundred and sixty three every person not being already ffree of this City occupying useing or exercising or who shall occupy use or exercise the Art Trade or Mistery of

Poulter within the City of London or Libertys thereof shall take upon himself and be admitted into the Ffreedom and be made a ffreeman of the said Company of the Master Wardens and Assistants of Poulters London And that no person or persons now using or exercising or who shall hereafter use or exercise the said Art Trade or Mistery of Poulter within the said Citie or Liberties thereof shall from and after the said Twenty fifth day of December be admitted by the Chamberlain of this City for the time being into the ffreedom or Liberties of this City of or in any other Company than the said Company of the Master Wardens and Assistants of Poulters London any Law Usage or custom of the City to the contrary notwithstanding Provided always that all and every person and persons not being already ffree of this City and who now are or hereafter shall be intitled to the ffreedom of any other Company within this City by Patrimony or Service and ought in pursuance of this Act to be made ffree of the said Company of the Master Wardens and Assistants of Poulters London shall be admitted into the ffreedom of the said Company upon payment of such and the like ffine and ffees and no more as are usually paid and payable upon admission of the child or apprentice of a ffreeman of the same Company into the ffreedom of the said Company And be it further enacted and ordained by the authority aforesaid that if any person (other than and except such persons as are already ffree of this City) do or shall at any time or times from and after the said Twenty fifth day of December occupy use or exercise the Art Trade or Mistery of Poulter within this City or Liberties thereof not being ffree of the said Company of the Masters Wardens and Assistants of Poulters London then every such person (other than and except as aforesaid) shall forfeit and pay the sum of Ffive pounds for every such offence

And be it further enacted and Ordained by the authority aforesaid That the fforfeitures and penalties made payable by this Act shall and may be recovered by action of debt Bill or Plaint to be commenced and prosecuted in the name of the Chamberlain of the said City of London for the time being with the privity and consent of the Master and Wardens of the said Company of Poulters in any of his Majestys Courts of Record to be holden within the said City Security being first given by the Master and Wardens of the said Company to indemnify the said Chamberlain against all costs damages and expenses that may happen or arise on account of commencing and prosecuting the said action And that the said Chamberlain of the said City for the time being in all Suits to be prosecuted by virtue of this present act against any offender shall recover his ordinary costs of suit to be expended in and about the prosecution of the same And that in case the said Chamberlain for the time being shall be Nonsuited or discontinue the said action or Judgment should be given against the said Chamberlain in any such action to be brought by virtue of this Act then the costs of such Nonsuit discontinuance or Judgment shall be paid and born by the Master Wardens and Assistants of Poulters London for the time being and the Chamberlain to be fully Indemnified and saved harmless by the said Master Wardens and Assistants of Poulters London of and from the same any Law usage or custom of the said City to the contrary notwithstanding And be it further enacted and ordained by the Authority aforesaid That all Penalties and fforfeitures to be had and recovered by Virtue of this Act (the charges of this Suit for the recovery thereof being first deducted) shall be divided into two equal parts the one moiety thereof shall be paid to the Treasuries of the Hospitals of Bridewell and Bethlem for the time being to be applied to the use of the incurables in the said Hospital of Bethlem only and the other Moiety thereof to him or them that shall prosecute the same

WILLIAM BROWNE Clerk of
   the Common Councel

HODGES

PASSED IN COMMON COUNCIL 22nd September 1820

An Act for explaining and amending an Act of Common Council made and passed the Twenty sixth of October one thousand seven hundred and sixty three intituled " An Act for regulating the Company of Poulters"

Whereas by an Act of Common Council made the Twenty sixth day of October One thousand seven hundred and sixty three intituled " An Act for regulating the Company of Poulters " It was among other things enacted ordained and established " That from and after the Twenty fifth
" day of December One thousand seven hundred and Sixty three any
" person not being then already Free of this City occupying using or
" exercising or who should occupy use or exercise the Art Trade or
" Mystery of Poulter within the City of London or Liberties thereof
" should take upon himself and be admitted into the Freedom and be
" made a Freeman of the Company of the Master Wardens and Assistants
" of Poulters London and that no person or Persons then using or
" exercising or who should thereafter use or exercise the Art Trade or
" Mystery of Poulter within the said City or Liberties thereof should from
" and after the said Twenty fifth day of December be admitted by the
" Chamberlain of the City for the time being into the Freedom or
" Liberties of this City of or in any other Company than the said Com-

"pany of Master Wardens and Assistants of Poulters London And it was
"thereby further enacted and ordained That if any Person (other than
"and except such persons as were then already free of this City) did or
"should at any Time or Times from and after the said Twenty fifth day
"of December occupy use or exercise the Art Trade or Mystery of
"Poulter within this City or Liberties thereof not being free of the said
"Company of the Master Wardens and Assistants of Poulters London
"then any such person (other than and except as aforesaid) should forfeit
"and pay the Sum of Five pounds for every such offence"

And Whereas It is expedient that the said Act of Common Councel made on the 26th day of October 1763 intituled an "Act for regulating the Company of Poulters" should be explained and amended so far as the same may affect or extend to or be deemed or construed to extend to Freemen of the several other companies of this City not having been admitted into the Freedom of the said Company of the Master Wardens and Assistants of Poulters London who act only as Salesmen Factors or Agents in the sale of Poultry Wares by wholesale in the public markets of this City and to such other person or persons being Freemen of this City who sell Poultry either by wholesale or Retail the same not being drawn trussed prepared or made fit and ready for dressing and not otherwise occupying using or exercising the Art Trade or Mystery of Poulter Be it therefore Enacted ordained Declared and Established by the Right Honourable the Lord Mayor the Right Worshipful his Brethren the Aldermen and Commons of this City in Common Council of this City and by authority of the same That from and after the passing of this Act the said Act of Common Council made and passed on the said Twenty sixth day of October One thousand seven hundred and sixty three intituled "An Act for regulating the Company of Poulters" and the Penalties thereby imposed or any clause matter or thing therein contained shall not extend or be deemed or construed to extend to any person who being a Freeman of this City in any other Company than the Company of the Master Wardens and Assistants of Poulters London either by Patrimony Apprenticeship or Redemption shall act as a Salesman Factor or Agent only in the Vend or Sale of any Poultry Wares by Wholesale in any of the Public Markets of this City or the Liberties thereof or to any person or persons being Freemen of this City who shall sell any Poultry either by Wholesale or Retail the same not being drawn Trussed prepared or made fit and ready for dressing and shall not otherwise occupy use or exercise the Art Trade or Mystery of Poulter; the said recited Act or any Law Usage or Custom of this City to the contrary notwithstanding.

Provided always and be it further enacted ordained and Established by the authority aforesaid That this Act or any thing therein contained shall not extend or be deemed or construed to extend to authorise allow permit or suffer any such Salesman Factor or Agent or any other person or persons whatsoever to occupy use or exercise otherwise than as such Salesman Factor or Agent or as such Seller of Poultry either by Wholesale or Retail the same not being drawn trussed prepared or made fit and ready for dressing the Art Trade or Mystery of Poulter in any of the Public markets or elsewhere within this City and the Liberties thereof not being free of the said Company of the Master Wardens and Assistants of Poulters London or in any other manner except as hereinbefore is Enacted Ordained Declared and Established contrary to the provisions true intent and meaning of the said recited Act of the Twenty sixth day of October One thousand seven hundred and sixty three **And be it further ordained and Established** by the authority aforesaid that if any such Salesman Factor or Agent or any such Seller of Poultry either by Wholesale or Retail the same not being drawn Trussed prepared or made fit and ready for dressing shall at any time from and after the passing of this Act occupy use or exercise otherwise than as aforesaid the Art Trade or Mystery of Poulter in any of the public Markets or elsewhere within this City and the Liberties thereof not being free of the said Company of Master Wardens and Assistants of Poulters London then every such person or persons shall forfeit and pay the sum of Five pounds for every such offence.

And be it further enacted ordained and established by the authority aforesaid That the forfeitures and Penalties imposed and made payable by this Act shall and may be recovered by action of Debt Bill or plaint to be commenced and prosecuted in the name of the Chamberlain of the City of London for the time being with the privity and consent of the Master and Wardens of the said Company of Poulters in any of His Majestys Courts of Record to be holden within the said City Security being first given by the said Master and Wardens of the said Company to indemnify the said Chamberlain against all costs damages and expenses that may happen to arise on account of commencing and prosecuting such action and that the said Chamberlain of the said City for the time being in all suits to be prosecuted by virtue of this present Act against any offender shall recover his ordinary Costs of Suit to be expended in and about the prosecution of the same and in case the said Chamberlain for the time being shall be Nonsuited or discontinue any such action or Judgment shall be given against the said Chamberlain in any such Action to be brought by virtue of this Act then the Costs of such Nonsuit Discontinuance or Judgment shall be borne and paid by the Master Wardens and Assistants of Poulters London and the Chamberlain to be fully indemnified and saved harmless by the said Master Wardens and Assistants of Poulters London of and from the same any Law usage or custom of the said City to the contrary notwithstanding

And be it further enacted ordained and established by the authority aforesaid that all penalties and forfeitures to be had and recovered by virtue of this Act (the charges for the Suit for the recovery thereof being first deducted) shall go and be applied in manner following that is to say one Moiety thereof to the use of the Master Wardens and Assistants of Poulters London and the other Moiety thereof to him or them that shall prosecute for the same

ESTATES AND CHARITIES.

LIST OF THE VARIOUS

ESTATES AND CHARITIES

BELONGING TO AND UNDER THE MANAGEMENT OF

The Worshipful Company of Poulters,

LONDON.

"NEPTON'S GIFT"

THOMAS NEPTON, by Will, dated 6th May, 1718, gave an Annuity of £20, to the Shoreditch Charity School, out of certain freehold property at Dunning's Alley, Bishopsgate; and, subject to such Annuity, gave all his freehold property to his Wife and her heirs. By a Deed, dated 22nd January, 1728, Ann Nepton, the Widow of the said Thomas Nepton, after leaving the property to various tenants for life, gave the freehold premises in Dunning's Alley to the Poulters' Company, Upon trust, to pay £40 per annum to certain poor persons belonging to the parish of Barking, Essex; and another £40 per annum to certain poor persons of the parish of St. Botolph, Aldgate; and, subject to the yearly payment to the Shoreditch School of £20, said Company were annually to pay one moiety of surplus rents, &c., for the use and benefit of such poor widows of freemen of the Company as should be necessitous, and the other moiety of surplus should be employed in placing out to be apprentices the children of such as should have been freemen of the Company and objects of charity, equally share and share alike so far as the residue of rents and profits should extend.

The property devised under this Will and Deed has sometime since been sold, and the produce thereof is now represented by various sums of Stock, invested in the Court of Chancery, the property having been conveyed to two Railway Companies, and the amount of Stock purchased is £11,889 16s. 5d. in the 3 per cent. Consols—namely, £3,287 13s. 5d. by the sale to the North London Railway Company, and £8,602 3s. to the Great Eastern Railway.

The net annual income received from Investment is about £356, exclusive of the dividends on accumulations of surplus moneys which now produce about £45.

The payments to Shoreditch School and the parishes of Barking and Aldgate are regularly made, as also to the Widows; but the disposition of the apprenticing portion of the Charity is the subject of Chancery proceedings for the purpose of arranging a Scheme for the more convenient disposition of the moiety of the surplus left for apprentices, by opening the same to the children of freemen of the City of London generally, there being a failure of objects meeting the exact requirements of the terms of the last-mentioned Settlement. There are now Eleven Widows receiving Pensions of various amounts.

"JOHN NEWMAN'S GIFT."

JOHN NEWMAN, by his Will, dated 11th August, 1727, devised (inter alia) a Messuage, in Budge Row, in the parish of St. Antholine, London, to certain tenants for life and their issue, and for want of such ssue, to the Poulters' Company and their Successors for ever, upon certain trusts particularly specified.

Owing to difficulties raised under the Will, the Estate became subject to various Chancery Suits, by divers persons claiming to be entitled to the property, and, ultimately, by Indentures of Lease and Release, of the 12th and 13th June, 1751, the property was formally conveyed to the Poulters' Company, by which the original trusts, created by the Testator, became wholly extinguished, and the premises have, ever since then, been in the undisturbed possession of the Poulters' Company.

The premises have, by Indenture of Lease, dated 12th July, 1870, been let to Mr. Daniel Davies, for a term of eighty years, from Lady Day, 1870, at an annual rent of £200 after the first twelve months, he having expended upwards of £3,500 in pulling down and rebuilding the premises.

The income derived from this property is received by the Poulters' Company for their own use and benefit.

"ROBERT WRIGHT'S GIFT."

ROBERT WRIGHT, by his Will, dated 16th April, 1548, reciting that he was possessed of a Rent Charge of 40s. per annum, issuing out of certain Lands, Houses, &c., lying in the west part of the parish of Allhallows, Lombard Street, gave the said Rent Charge for ever to the Parson and Churchwardens of the said Parish, and their Successors, to the intent that out of 20s. parcel thereof, they should yearly, and for ever, pay to the Wardens of his Company of Poulters the annual rent of 17s. 6d., for the helping and succouring of the necessitous of the said Company, when they should happen to be called to any charge; and the other 2s. 6d. of the same, he gave to the said Parson and Churchwardens for their pains in that behalf to be taken, that is to say, to every of them 6d.; and he directed that, if the said Parson and Churchwardens should be negligent in performing his desire, that the said Company of Poulters should have the rent charge of 40s., to the intent aforesaid, and, if it should come to the hands, and they should afterwards be found remiss in executing the trust, the said annual rent should return again to the said Parson and Churchwardens.

The sum of 17s. 6d., is annually paid by the Churchwardens of the parish of Allhallows, Lombard Street, to the Company in respect of this donation, which sum is paid half-yearly at Midsummer and Christmas to a Pensioner of this Company as a gift of the Testator.

"*JONATHAN BROWNE'S GIFT.*"

JONATHAN BROWNE, by his Will dated 18th October, 1704, gave to the Company £50, to be by them put out at interest, and the produce thereof to be paid to the poor of the said Company, by equal portions, on each Whitsunday or Christmas-day, for ever.

This sum of £50 was received by the Company from MR. BROWNE'S Executors, in two payments of £25 each, viz., on 13th November, 1705, and 3rd February, 1706; but it does not appear to have been invested by the Company in Government Securities until 14th September, 1725, as no item of account of the purchase of Stock appears in the Company's book, until that time, when the Company seem to have laid out £123 9s. 6d. in the purchase of South Sea Stock, but what amount of Stock that sum purchased is not stated; but it is presumed to have been £100 Stock, as the price of Stock (appears by papers published on 18th September, 1725) was £121 and a quarter; if so, the proportion belonging to this Charity would be £40 13s., and the interest thereon would be £1 5s. 6d.

The Company appears to have regularly paid £5 per cent. interest on this £50 amongst the poor, in the name of the Testator, by payments of £1 5s. half-yearly, until the 7th February, 1734; but it has been paid for many years to a Pensioner of the Company, half-yearly, at Midsummer and Christmas, by even payments of 12s. 9d. each.

"JAMES SMITH'S GIFT."

JAMES SMITH, a Freeman of the Company, by his Will dated 21st April, 1731, gave to the Master Wardens and Assistants of the Company of Poulters, and their Successors, a yearly rent of £10, issuing out of certain Messuages, Lands, &c., situate in the parish of Potton, in the county of Bedford, on Trust, that they should twice in every year, in

June and December for ever, distribute the said yearly Rent, towards the relief and support of such poor men, free of the said Company, or the Widows of such Freemen, in such manner, and in proportion, as they in their discretion should think fit.

The property upon which this Rent charge is secured, is now in possession of Geo. Smith, Esquire—and the Company receive, and always received, the Annuity of £10 clear regularly; but the present tenant deducts property tax.

This sum has been for many years paid by the Company, quarterly, to two Pensioners specifically, as the gift of the Testator.

"ROBERT SMITH'S GIFT."

ROBERT SMITH, late citizen and Poulter of London, by his Will dated 22nd February, 1737, gave to the Master, Wardens, and Assistants of Poulters, London, and their Successors, the sum of £250 in Trust, that they should place the same out at interest, on Government or other good security, and distribute the yearly interest towards the relief and support of such poor Freemen of the said Company, or the Widows of such Freemen, as they in their discretion should think fit.

This Legacy was received by the Company from Mr. Smith's Executors, on the 2nd February, 1739, as appears by the Books. It also appears by the Books that, in the said month of February, 1739, the Company laid out £331 10s. in the purchase of £300 South Sea Stock, which (it is imagined) was made up of this £250 of Robert Smith's, and £81 10s. the Company's own monies, instead of their purchasing a fraction of Stock with the £250.

According to the price of Stock at that time, the £250 belonging to Mr. Robert Smith was laid out; the proportion belonging to that Charity is £226 4s. 11d., the interest arising from which would be £6 15s. 4d. This Trust Fund is now consolidated, like the other Charities, in the Company's Funds; but the dividends on the said sum of Stock are duly paid, quarterly, to Two Pensioners of the Company specifically in the Testator's name.

"OZELL PITT'S GIFT."

OZELL PITT, by his Will, the date of which does not appear, gave to the Company of Poulters £50, 5 per cent. annuities to be purchased by his Executor, and transferred to the Company, and to be by them held in Trust, to pay the Dividends half-yearly to the Six Lower Pensioners of the Company.

This sum of £50 Navy per cents. was transferred, by Mr. Pitt's Executors, to the Company, and remained standing, with £50 of their own money, like Stock, until the Navy 5 per cents. were reduced by Act of Parliament to 4 per cent. Stock, and afterwards further reduced to 3½ per cent. After this reduction, it was thought best by the Court, as the Company had no other Stock but this £100 3½, to sell the same out, and that it should form one fund by adding the same to their own South Sea Stock. Accordingly, on the 30th March, 1831, this £100, 3½ per cents., was sold out, and produced the sum of £87 2s. 6d., money; and, on 6th September, 1831, the Company purchased £100 South Sea Stock for £81 2s. 6d., so that the proportion Stock belonging to this Charity (allowing for difference in price) would be £45 11s. 3d., the interest upon which is £1 8s. 6d. The Pension being so small, the income is distributed half-yearly to One Pensioner only, by payments of 14s. 3d. each, at Midsummer and Christmas.

"ROBERT WARDEN'S GIFT."

ROBERT WARDEN, Citizen and Poulter, by his Will, bearing date 3rd June, 1609, gave to the Company a house, then known by the sign of the Pepper Queen, in the Parish of St. Peter, Cornhill, on condition that they should pay to the Parson and Churchwardens of the Parish yearly £3 12s.; whereof 52s. should be bestowed, by twelve pence, every Sunday, in Bread; and, in case any Freeman of the said Company should inhabit in the said Parish, and should be needful to be relieved, he should have a rateable share; the residue to be bestowed for two Sermons, to be preached in the Parish Church, one on Ash Wednesday, and the other on the 10th of March, yearly.

Instead of Two Sermons, there is now only one preached, namely that on Ash Wednesday.

The house devised is situate at the corner of Cornhill and Bishopsgate Street, and is in the occupation of Mr. Alderman Carter, a Chronometer Maker, at £150 per annum, on Lease—which will expire at Michaelmas, 1888. In addition, Mr. Carter has to pay a Rent, in lieu of insurance, on the value of £1,200.

The Annuity has been regularly paid by the Company.

Since 1773, it has been increased, and the payments are now made as follows:—

Minister of St. Peter's, for Sermon.	£2	2	0
Poor of St. Peter's, including £1 given by Court	3	12	6
Parish Clerk, 7s.; Organist, 10s.; Sexton, 8s.; Organ Blower, 2s.; and Beadle, 2s. 6d.	1	9	6
Charity Children, about.	0	18	6
Together	£8	2	6

LONDON :

PRINTED BY W. H. AND L. COLLINGRIDGE,

CITY PRESS, ALDERSGATE STREET.

www.ingramcontent.com/pod-product-compliance
Lightning Source LLC
Chambersburg PA
CBHW020301090426
42735CB00009B/1173